"*Keven's Choice* is a pr
—a searingly honest p................. .. .., ...,
relate to. This book will provide solace and inspiration to countless readers. It's about substance use and being a parent. Ultimately, it's about love."

DAVID SHEFF, *NEW YORK TIMES*
BESTSELLING AUTHOR OF *BEAUTIFUL BOY*
AND *CLEAN*

"*Keven's Choice* is a heartbreaking story about loving someone with substance use disorder. Legere's remarkable work leaves you with a deeper appreciation of life's blessings."

ED KRESSY, PROFESSIONAL SPEAKER AND
AUTHOR OF *MY ADDICTION & RECOVERY*

BARBARA LEGERE

KEVEN'S CHOICE

A Mother's Journey Through Her Son's
Mental Illness, Addiction and Suicide

ISBN: 979-8-9852253-3-4 (e-book)

ISBN: 978-1-956955-13-2 (paperback)

CONTENTS

This book is dedicated to Maggie Fleitman and the memory of her precious son, Mitchell

AUTHOR'S NOTE

In an effort to reduce the stigma against people who struggle with substance use, the word "addiction" is used minimally in this book. In its place, I use the term "Substance Use Disorder" (SUD) and "substance users" to replace "addicts."

Most names have been changed with the exception of those of my family and closest friends.

What if we replaced the word "addict" with: "A human being who suffered so much that he or she finds in drugs or some other behavior a temporary escape from that suffering"?
~Dr. Gabor Maté

INTRODUCTION

My son Keven and I often talked about writing a book together. Then a few months after he died, I was faced with writing it alone. Keven and I wanted to share encouragement and hope for those struggling with co-occurring substance use and mental health issues and their families. He always thought of this book as his "happy ending." Sadly, Keven did not have a happy ending, but his journey mattered. His life mattered, and the events leading to his death contain a serious message for every family.

Keven was my only child. He took his life after battling substance abuse for many years. He was tortured by the voices in his head telling him he was worthless and a loser. Keven's heart was full of love for his family and his friends—but not for himself.

As parents, most of us would do anything to save our child from the outcome Keven suffered. Did I fail my son? Could I have saved him? What would have made a difference? Was he failed by the systems that are intended to help people with mental illness and Substance Use Disorder (SUD)? And what about those who belittled him and looked down on him because of his disease? Why is it called a disease when so many treat it as a moral failing or a character defect? Why do insurance companies treat SUD differently from other deadly diseases?

These are some of the things I talk about within these pages. I don't have all the answers; I have the story of one young man, and his experience isn't unique—there are hundreds of thousands like him suffering from SUD in our country and many who are losing their lives to it. This book was not easy to write, but I want Keven's story to be of help. By sharing my son with you, I hope to bring to light foundational dangers that render countless lives lost to opiate overdose and suicide.

Some of these dangers are:

- the social stigma associated with substance use and mental illness
- the greed and failures inherent in the drug and recovery community
- the indifference and inaction by government officials who allow drugs to cross our borders
- the judgments of our society and culture that cause pain and feelings of hopelessness
- the newest danger to the current generation of young people: fentanyl

I believe that real change starts with a few people and then spreads outward in ripples—or waves—that can eventually impact the world. I hope my journey and the lessons I've learned along the way will encourage you to reach out to someone who is suffering. After all, a little kindness goes a long way. Compassion and understanding aren't just niceties—they have the power to give hope. Countless human beings are struggling every day not to use drugs. They are trying to find real help, and they want to believe in themselves. They need us.

I love you, Keven; you are forever in my heart. Your life mattered.

CHAPTER 1
MY TROUBLED SON

> *Mental pain is less dramatic than physical pain, but it is*
> *more common and also more hard to bear. The frequent*
> *attempt to conceal mental pain increases the burden: it is*
> *easier to say "My tooth is aching" than to say "My heart*
> *is broken."*
>
> ~C. S. Lewis, *The Problem of Pain*

Two years before he died, my only child sat next to me in the morning sun as I sipped my coffee. Our yard was filled with plants and colorful flowers, and I had that content, comfortable feeling moms get sometimes—a moment of harmonious silence and companionship with your kid at your side. That peace didn't last long.

"Mom, we need to talk." Keven lit up a Marlboro Smooth and turned to me with a serious expression. I prepared myself for something upsetting.

"Will you please tell me it's okay if I kill myself?"

My chest tightened, a familiar churning starting in my gut. Suicide was a common discussion in our house. Keven had attempted it many times, and each time he had asked me not to revive him if I found him. I always had. What parent wouldn't?

"Honey—" I tried to argue. Like usual.

Keven grabbed my hand. "Mom, look at me. You know how fucking unhappy I am. I don't have any real friends. I can't get a job. I can't stop using. I'm tired of feeling all this anxiety. All I want to do is die." His eyes watery, he looked away. Except for crows squawking overhead, it was quiet.

"Please, just tell me it's okay if I kill myself. I'm not saying I'll do it today or in the near future. I don't know if I'll ever get the nerve up, but if I ever do, I need to know you'll understand. I know you don't want me to, but I need to know you'll get over it."

In the eight-hour conversation that followed, I crossed back and forth between feelings and logic. I felt like a failure as a parent. Logically, I knew I had done everything possible to help him, using every resource available to me. Keven was raised with unconditional love, and we were exceptionally close. I knew he loved me. The one thought I kept returning to: *I'm his mom. I should be able to prevent this.*

I looked away. Except for a few years in my 20s, I had lived in this house since I was 10 years old. Keven had lived here since the day he was born. The large yard had old-growth trees that provided welcome shade on hot afternoons. The pond that my dad lovingly created rippled near our chairs. A few years back, Keven decided we needed a waterfall, so he designed one himself and got it installed. Beautiful rocks gently descended into the pool, where bright koi swam endlessly in circles with nowhere to go.

That was how Keven felt. He was stuck, and he longed to be free of the pain that was his life.

I looked into his glassy eyes, grateful to see the emotion that told me he wasn't *too* high; he'd only used just enough heroin to avoid withdrawal symptoms. He was wearing shorts, and I placed my hand on his knee; his skin was warm from the sun. Both of his legs were covered with scars from the infections he got from shooting up. But I loved every inch of him, all of his scars—inside and out.

"Kev, I will never give you permission to kill yourself. I'll do anything to help you—anything—but I can't lose you. You're the most important person in my life. You *are* my life!"

"Look, Mom, you know how much I love you. I don't want to hurt you. Please, just agree to it," he argued. That's what substance users do. They argue until they wear you down.

I became irritated because I recognized that I was in for a long day of this, and I just wanted to enjoy this beautiful moment with Keven. The sun. The pond. The flowers. Like always, it was tempting to just agree so we could move on, but this was one battle he was going to lose. What parent would give their child permission to kill themself?

My mind sorted through all the mental files I had stored from similar conversations over the years, searching for encouraging words—something that might work to change Keven's mind, to remind him of all the ways he was loved, of why he was loved. I had nothing new to say, nothing new to try. It seemed like we were out of resources and methods for recovery.

Sometimes I'd find Keven passed out on his bedroom floor after using heroin and Xanax together. If his breathing was strong, I'd grab my pillow so I could lie down next to him to keep watch. I would have to clear a spot on the floor, which was typically littered with his clothes—clean and dirty mixed together. I would lay my hand across his chest to feel his lungs working. Sometimes I'd pray. Other times I'd just think: *What more can I do? What the hell more can I do?*

If I found Keven unconscious, I'd try to revive him while calling 911. I kept NARCAN—a medication that reverses opioid overdoses in just minutes—in the house for that reason. It comes as a nasal spray and also in a form that can be injected. I had both. Once revived at home or in the hospital, Keven would be upset that he was still alive.

Keven's first few suicide attempts landed him in the hospital's "Behavioral Health" department. They would keep him there for the standard 72-hour psychiatric hold (known as a

"5150") and put him on an ever-evolving cocktail of psychiatric meds. (I used to think "5150" was just the name of a Van Halen album; I know better now, but I wish I didn't.)

So suicide was not a new subject in our house. On this otherwise beautiful morning, I was tempted to reach over and run my fingers through Kev's thick hair. He hadn't used hair gel today, and it looked soft and natural like when he was a kid—back when he would ask me to play with his hair. I wanted to cradle him in my arms, sing to him and promise him everything would be okay—like moms do.

But recently, Keven had become averse to being touched, so I had to hold myself back from placing a comforting hand on his arm or rubbing his neck and shoulders. He would only allow me to hug him if I asked. I wanted to soothe him but held back to be respectful.

It was exhausting to tread so carefully around things that might trigger his anger or a deeper depression. Like everyone, after a long day I only wanted to relax, but determining Keven's mood often felt like a second job. I couldn't let my guard down. I had to stay alert and watch my words.

I eventually learned never to ask Keven if he wanted to go to detox or rehab. Instead, I'd wait for him to ask. He would sometimes go just to please me and give me hope, knowing full well that he wasn't ready to stop using. And any conversation about his future brought on depression, so I never broached the subject.

"Sweetheart, I know how much you're suffering, and I swear to God, the universe and on my father's grave that I would take your pain if I could. If cutting off a limb would make it all go away, I'd do it now." I had fantasies about it. In my imagination, I'd see Kev standing next to a beautiful young woman. Both were smiling, and I was smiling up at them from my wheelchair with one leg missing. Kev would lean over and hand me his newborn baby. I'd catch myself smiling at the thought of this perfect solution until the current cold reality settled back in.

Keven lit his third cigarette, and I was ready to get some housework done. He surprised me by hugging me tight as we stood to go into the house. "I love you so much, Mom. I'm sorry I'm such a fucked-up burden to you." The words stung because no child is ever a burden to their parents. Some just require more work than others.

He was wearing a red Rage Against the Machine T-shirt. At 6'1", he was the perfect height for my head to rest on his shoulder. Childhood memories played in my mind. What happened to my smiling son, the one with an insatiable curiosity, full of laughter and silliness? Keven was endlessly lovable. He was kind, generous and compassionate. He had a quirky sense of humor and was loved by kids and the elderly alike. I savored this moment in his arms.

Keven followed me around as I took care of the day's mundane chores. While I was at the sink doing dishes, he leaned his long torso on the counter, talking more about his need for me to let him kill himself. I ran the vacuum, which brought me some quiet, but when I moved on to laundry, he followed me up and down the stairs and out into the garage. No matter how mad I got, Keven would not let up. He waited outside the bathroom as I showered. He was relentless.

"Can I make you some lunch?" I asked, hoping it would distract him. Keven said no and grabbed a Recovery Rockstar from the fridge. I couldn't eat either; my stomach was upset. I lay down for a while, hoping he'd give me a break and stop nagging. He sat on the edge of my bed, holding our dog, Sugar, loving on her while I pretended to sleep.

As soon as I opened my eyes, Keven started in again. I begged him to stop, to leave me alone. I would never agree. I was angry. He was wearing me down. These long, drawn-out rants were usually his way of getting me to give in about money or use of my car. When my aggravation level was just about to the point of an explosion, I'd yell, "Okay!" He knew my weaknesses and played them well. Substance users do.

Then, as the morning hours warmed into the afternoon and then cooled into evening, I lost my will. After all, they were just words, right? I gave Keven what he wanted.

"Fine, Keven. I give you my permission to end your life." I was too numb to cry, too defeated to argue. The words rang in my ears.

"Thank you, Mom. Thank you, thank you! You have no idea how much this means to me. I don't want to die with you mad at me." Keven smiled as if I'd handed him a longed-for gift; keys to the car or concert tickets for Linkin Park.

I cried myself to sleep that night, staring at the ceiling and asking out loud, "What have I done?"

If he did do it, I would blame myself, and that wasn't what he was after. For years, I had been arguing with myself as I tossed and turned at night, never knowing which voice to listen to. One side accused me of being responsible for Keven's issues; the other side defended me because I couldn't stand the thought that I had caused his misery. The debate on nurture versus nature meant that no matter what I thought caused Keven's problems, I could be blamed. Whenever I caught myself stuck in this way of thinking, I'd force the negative thoughts out and tell myself that I was a good mother. My mistakes were made in love. I first understood true love when I became Keven's mother, and I knew that if love were enough to heal Substance Use Disorder, Keven's torture should have ended as soon as it began.

For weeks after our conversation, I jumped at any unexpected sounds. I had always been nervous and on edge in the 10 years Keven had been using, but now it was at a whole new level. I tried to keep tabs on him when he left the house. When he was alone in his room, I'd listen at the door and knock if I didn't hear him moving around.

Being on alert for an accidental overdose is typical for any parent of a heroin user. You're always waiting for "the call." If Keven wasn't home and the phone rang late at night, I'd jump out of my skin with worry. The sound of sirens in the distance

sent up alarm bells. The typical parental worries of horrible acci-
dents or your child being arrested had happened on more than
one occasion, but we had always gotten through it. This time, I
wasn't so sure.

Suicide is final. And I was tortured by the idea that I had cut
the one string to life that Keven had: me.

I had been losing Keven in incremental ways over his years
of using drugs. But Keven was crazy if he thought I'd get over
losing him permanently!

As the days and weeks passed, I gradually let down my
guard and settled back into my normal level of worry and
distress. But every morning began with me wondering whether
Keven was alive and whether today could be his final day on
earth.

As for Keven, he never brought up our conversation again,
but my instincts to worry were right because the day I gave my
son permission to die, the timer started on his life. Substance use
can kill you slowly or quickly. Keven and I would only have two
more years.

CHAPTER 2
AN UNEXPECTED LIFE

A baby fills the place in your heart you never knew was empty.

~Anonymous

"You just got pregnant." An announcement rang inside my head on March 3, 1990 at 11:30 pm. Was it the voice of God? My intuition? I only knew that I believed it.

Jim and I had met several years earlier when his best friend, Tom, and my best friend, Kathy, asked us to be their best man and maid of honor. They introduced Jim and me a few months prior to the big day, and we hit it off and started dating. I was 27, and Jim was 30, and despite some good times, we split up after three years. Then about a year later, we got together one night for "pizza and a few beers," and as exes often do, we ended up at his place.

As I got ready to leave, I blurted out, "I just got pregnant!" and told him about the voice in my head. His reaction surprised me; he took in my expression but didn't challenge my news.

"Okay," he said, "well, let me know when you find out for sure."

I tried desperately to put the thought of being pregnant out of my mind. The voice must have been my imagination. But after two weeks of obsessing, I had to find out if it was true. Not trusting an over-the-counter test, I met with my doctor and expressed to her how much I did not want a baby. This was not in my plans.

I sat in the exam room looking at the photos on the wall of embryos growing into fetuses, then full-grown babies. The room was cold, and the wait was an eternity.

When the door finally opened, my doctor surprised me. "Good news," she said. "Your urine test is negative. We'll take a blood sample just to be sure, but I don't think you have anything to worry about." Relief flooded over me. I had been given my life back! I thanked her and walked out of the office, feeling like I'd been handed a gift. The voice in my head was just my mind playing tricks on me.

A few days later, my doctor called me at work, reversing my relief. "No! No!" I screamed into the phone, my voice carrying through the office. A co-worker came running to see what was wrong.

"What happened? Is it your mom?" she asked with genuine concern.

"I need to leave; tell my boss I had an emergency." I grabbed my purse, got on the elevator, and tried to hold my tears in. I sat in my car in the parking structure and cried until I was calm enough to drive.

Heading toward Jim's house, my imagination saw Jim smiling at the news and giving me a big hug. "I hope it's a boy," he'd say. I'd smile and reply, "My intuition says it is!" We'd sit down over a glass of iced tea and discuss the future of our child, who would live with me full-time, but Jim could see him every weekend if he wanted. We would amicably share holidays. Jim would happily pay a fair amount of child support; we wouldn't even need to make it official by going through the court system. Our son would grow up knowing he was loved by both parents and extended families.

Then logic set in. It was more likely that Jim would be flustered and upset. As a decent guy, he'd feel obligated to ask me to marry him. In that case, the answer would be "No." I wasn't in love with him, and he wasn't in love with me. Later, I'd wonder if it would have been better for Keven if we'd married so he could be raised by both parents. Guilt would nag at me, but I believe I made the right decision. Jim and I were very different from each other, and marriage should be based on love, not obligation.

As I pulled up in front of his house, Jim was out front washing his truck with his shirt off. He worked construction and was a surfer. He had long blond hair, a bronze body, sea-blue eyes and a beautiful smile.

Jim looked up as my car pulled in front of his house. He turned off the hose and walked toward me. I could see in his eyes he knew why I was here.

"So, you're pregnant?" He raised his eyebrows as he asked.

"Yep." We stood there staring at each other.

"So, what's the plan?" he asked.

"I'm having the baby." At some point during the drive, I'd decided not to end this pregnancy. I'd had an abortion in my early teens out of fear and desperation, and even though this time a baby still wasn't in my life plans, I'd do my best to be a wonderful mom.

"Well, we could get married," he said, just as I knew he would. Now there was fear in those blue eyes. I hesitated, letting him sit in his discomfort. When I declined, I watched relief sweep across his face. But what came next surprised me and hit like a punch to the gut.

"Promise me something—you will never tell my family."

What the heck? I wasn't expecting to hear this at all. I understood he didn't love me, but we were friends, and this was his child! Why would he want to deprive this baby of his family? I loved his parents and his siblings; we had always got along well. How dare he not want his family to know! I was hurt and angry. Rather than ask why, I blurted out, "Okay, if that's what you want, I won't say a word." I was too proud to put up an argument.

If this was how Jim felt, he didn't deserve to be part of the baby's life. It crushed my heart to hear these words leave his mouth. Jim's handsomeness turned ugly to me at that moment. No, I hadn't planned on this kid, but I didn't want to deprive him of half of his family or them of him. My family, although wonderful, was smaller and didn't have the big, happy-family vibe that Jim's had with aunts, uncles and cousins his age. Nothing more was said. I turned away and walked to my car.

Jim had married straight out of high school and quickly had a daughter, Annie. She lived with her maternal grandparents about an hour away. During my years with Jim, Annie and I had become close. She was a teenager now, and I knew she'd love having a younger sibling. Jim didn't see Annie too often. It would be hard for me not to tell her because we kept in touch by phone and sometimes letters. How could I deprive my baby of a relationship with a sibling?

Keven and Annie

It occurred to me a few days later why Jim didn't want me to tell his parents. They'd badger him to be a responsible father, which included paying child support. I hadn't asked for financial help from him—I hadn't even thought that far in the future; this was all so new! It was either that or he didn't think of the baby as our child; he thought of it as my child. Or maybe it was both. I agreed to his terms. It was my way of telling him I didn't need him; I could raise this child without his involvement.

Years later I did ask for child support and regretted that we didn't sit down and discuss this after we both had time to adjust to the idea that we were bringing a child into the world. Maybe then we could have avoided the eventual involvement of the courts. There is just no way of predicting what you will need as a parent until you become one.

Within a few years, Jim was married and expecting his third child with his new wife, Cindy. At that point, he started coming by about once a month to see Keven—taking him to the park, buying him birthday and Christmas gifts. I never asked but have always had the feeling that Cindy may have influenced Jim to be part of Kev's life. Jim was a pilot and had a small plane at a local airport. He would often ask Keven to go help him work on the plane. I don't think they ever actually flew in it, but I know Keven enjoyed helping his dad with this project.

I noticed that the older Keven got, the easier it was for Jim to communicate with him. By the time Keven was an adult, he had a good relationship with his dad and saw him, Cindy and his half-brother Josh often.

Telling my own family about the pregnancy helped me feel more confident about my decision. My mother and sister were sitting at the kitchen table when I walked into the house. "I have something to tell you guys." I paused for a moment. It was clear by my facial expression that it wasn't good news. "I'm pregnant." As soon as the words came out, I felt tears forming but held them in.

The first words out of my mom were, "How could you be so

stupid?" followed immediately by, "It will be great to have a new baby in the family!"

My sister Therese was thrilled. It was an enormous relief that they were both happy with the news, and I felt relieved and ready to begin this new phase with their love and support.

At this time, my mom, sister and I were all living together. We got along fine for the most part, but there had always been an underlying tension between my mom and me. Ever since I was a young child, I sensed a distance between us that I didn't understand until adulthood. She didn't know what to do with a daughter who was so different than her. My mom grew up during the Depression, and although her family was well off, she saw hardships. She had a domineering mother and did what she was told, never questioning or disagreeing with anyone. She was a realist. I, on the other hand, questioned everything and was a dreamer. I spent more time in my imagination than reality.

Mom had no expectations of her children going to college or pursuing specific careers; she just wanted us to be happy. I never went to college—instead, I worked full-time and partied every weekend. My plans for the future were to build a career working for the Warmington Company—a successful real estate development company—eventually working my way up to being a Project Manager for Land Use Planning. My other goal was to have as much fun as possible while not working. This didn't sit well with my mother who didn't understand why I had to "go out all the time." Like most moms, she preferred me staying at home.

I cried for weeks after initially learning I was pregnant. After all, I was happy with the way things were. I didn't want to give up my lifestyle, and my life as I knew it was over. It didn't occur to me that life as a mother could be the best thing that had ever happened to me. I was also nervous about going into single parenting not knowing a thing. I eventually shed my fears as my belly grew with new life. My lack of readiness was slowly evolving into acceptance, then excitement. We were going to be okay!

Then, eight months into my pregnancy, the owner of the Warmington Company stepped into my office. He wanted to talk.

Why would Bob Warmington want to talk to me? I'd never been called into his office in the five years I was employed there. I really cared for Bob because Bob really cared for his employees. He was genuine and sincere in all of his business dealings, so while I was curious, I wasn't worried.

Bob was from a prominent family in Orange County and was known for his love of the arts, philanthropy and ethical business practices. My nerves were calm as I stepped into the warmth of his office. In the middle of the room was an enormous crackling fireplace where we would gather for company meetings, referred to as "fireside chats." He motioned for me to sit on the forest green couch and offered me a cup of tea.

"Barbara, I hate to say it, but the industry has taken a tremendous hit. In the next six months, we're going to start layoffs, and I can't promise that your job will be safe. You're ready to give birth, so I'm offering you the option of leaving now with a bonus." Bob's eyes teared up.

My mind was racing. What should I do? I would never have a job like this again—the perks of the job were unbelievable! We had an on-site gym with a pool where the Men's USA Water Polo Team worked out. They played basketball on our indoor court, and if we didn't feel like using the facilities ourselves, we could at least watch. There were yearly retreats—week-long, all-expense-paid vacations in addition to our personal time off— tropical get-aways to places like The Bahamas or Hawaii. There was nothing like sipping a Mai Tai on the beach with your co-workers musing, "I'm getting paid for this!"

Occasionally, Bob would close the office early and take us out on his yacht for a cruise off the coast of Newport Beach. And the Christmas parties! Elegant, extravagant and entertaining, they always showed up in the society pages of the local newspaper. The Warmington Company exemplified the adage, "happy workers work harder."

Bob interrupted my thoughts. "The bonus amount is $10,000, and I will continue to pay your full salary, insurance included, for the next six months." I understood he was offering me a generous gift and knew that my job would most likely be eliminated if I didn't accept this offer. I accepted. Although I didn't want to lose the job, this offer meant I would be paid while staying home with my baby for six months. I'd get to spend time with him and experience all the sweetness of being a new mom.

The first week not working felt like a holiday. The second week felt like I was missing out on something. By the third week, I was lamenting the loss of my future. I had planned on working at the Warmington Company for as long as they'd have me. It was my co-workers that I missed the most, as they had become good friends in and outside the office.

A month after losing my job, Keven was born. He had refused to reveal his gender during the ultrasounds, but I knew he was a boy. In the last month of pregnancy, the name I had chosen didn't seem to fit—Daniel or Dan or Danny. Then one day, the name Kevin came to me but didn't feel perfect until I changed it to Keven with an "e."

In 1990, it was "a thing" to go through childbirth with no drugs. The pain of a drug-free birth was somehow supposed to prove you were a "real woman." My labor lasted over 20 hours, and naturally, there were times I wanted to jump out the hospital window to escape the pain. Finally going into active labor, I pushed for two hours. In true Keven style, he wasn't ready on time. The nurses told me the baby's heartbeat was too high, which led to an emergency C-section.

My OB-GYN was a frumpy guy in his 40s who had the personality of a wet napkin. When Keven was delivered, he incoherently mumbled the gender as if no one would care.

"What? What is it?" I yelled. Still lying on my back with the

surgical drape separating me from the baby, I had to know if I
was right. Was it a boy?

A nurse shouted, "Congratulations, you have a boy!" On
December 7, 1990, Keven David Legere entered the world.

Therese was by my side the entire time and held Keven even
before I did. Lying on the surgery table, I was shaking—weak
and worn out. Therese placed Keven in my arms. Holding my
son for the first time, marveling at that sweet little face, I was in
awe. He was perfect in every way. Holding my eight-pound
bundle of wonder, I felt like a pioneer about to embark on an
expedition to an unknown and mysterious land: excited and
determined to give it my all.

Therese, my mother and I brought Keven home to a house
full of love. He would bring us more joy—and more heartbreak
—than we ever could have imagined.

Even though I had kept my promise to Jim to never reveal his
secret son, fate intervened two years later when I saw Jim's
sister, Lisa, at the park where I'd taken Keven to play. He was 18
months old, happily running around as I sat nearby watching.
Lisa took one look at him and exclaimed, "That's Jimmy's kid!"
She had her two-year-old son with her.

I explained to Lisa how Jim had forced me to keep Keven a
secret from his family. She took care of that for me. Lisa was so
thrilled that she bought a bottle of champagne and drove to her
parents' house to share the good news. They were ecstatic and
called me to plan a party to welcome Keven into their family.

Keven loved his grandparents. On holidays, he'd spend the
mornings at home with my family and me, then go spend time
with his dad's side of the family. It meant a lot to him to be
included. Their relationship was cemented from the beginning,
and Jim's family always stayed supportive. When he was old
enough to drive, Kev would show up at their house unan-
nounced for afternoon visits. They told me they loved opening
the door to find him there. He was an excellent conversationalist
(even when high), and they loved him so deeply that I doubt

they ever realized that sometimes when he stopped by, he had been using. Even as his substance use increased over the years, if his grandparents knew about it, they never said a word. They were a happy couple who loved family above all else and were a blessing to Keven. He never felt different—they treated him like all the other grandkids. I will be forever grateful for their positive influence on Keven's life.

I couldn't have predicted that being a mother would be the greatest joy of my life. Like a lot of unprepared mothers-to-be, I worried about all the usual things: losing my freedom, changing my lifestyle and ruining my friendships and social life. I cried every day at work and at home. Did Keven sense this from the womb? Were my selfish, negative thoughts the reason he felt unworthy and not good enough? These questions haunt me to this day. Even though he was showered with unconditional love all his life, were my anxious thoughts and worries during pregnancy the cause of Keven's unhappiness in life?

CHAPTER 3
FAMILY

> *Only an aunt can give hugs like a mother, keep secrets like a sister and love like a friend.*
> ~Anonymous

Therese was more than an aunt to Keven. She had a unique relationship with him. Sometimes they were more like siblings, arguing and teasing each other. Keven always knew which buttons to push to get his aunt "T" upset. They had their own language, calling each other "Goat Roper" and "Pig Licker." I thought these were bizarre names, then found out years later that this was an inside joke from the movie *Joe Dirt*.

Every spring break, T would take us on a week-long road trip vacation. Half the fun was getting there. We visited Zion and Bryce in Utah, the Grand Canyon in Arizona and Yosemite closer to home here in California. We agreed that hiking in the snow was so much more fun than hiking on dirt—the crisp air tickling our throats, snow crunching under our boots, cold cheeks tingling.

Keven would be in the backseat, usually talking non-stop. We'd play the typical road games. His favorite was counting specific types of cars.

"Let's count Lamborghinis now," Keven suggested playfully in the middle of the Utah desert. "Um, let's not and say we did," Therese shot back. So it was back to counting Fords and Nissans.

On one occasion while driving home from Arizona, Keven begged Therese to put the pedal to the metal and see how fast her new Toyota Highlander would go. He reasoned that we were in the middle of nowhere and hadn't seen another car in over an hour; plus, it was a straight road. The moment she hit 100 mph, red and blue lights and a loud siren came out of nowhere. Oops, we'd forgotten the area was patrolled by some sort of magical radar where invisible cops lie in wait for speed demons.

Keven was wearing sunglasses, a beanie with a skull and crossbones pattern, a leather bracelet with spikes and a necklace with mini brass knuckles (all purchased at a souvenir shop on our trip). When the officer approached the car, Keven spoke to him in a confident and adult voice from the passenger seat.

"Officer, I apologize. It was my fault she was driving so fast. We just bought this car, and I convinced her to break it in by giving it a little gas for a few minutes."

The officer was wearing mirrored sunglasses, and his expression was hard to read. He was holding a ticket pad and pen in his hands. He looked at Therese, me and then Keven. "All right, sir, just a warning this time, but keep to the speed limit from here on out," he said directly to Kev. Once he had driven off, we all whooped and hollered, praising Keven for pulling this off. I felt proud of him for his maturity rather than being alarmed at his growing skills for manipulation. We laughed about it for years, but this was an early indication of how convincing Keven could be when he wanted things his way.

Therese was like a friend to Keven. She hung out with him and his friends in his room, watching *SpongeBob* and *The Simpsons*. So, when the time came to buy a car when Kev was in his teens, Therese helped. If he chose something that I couldn't afford, Therese offered to pay the difference. I still have a deep appreciation for her relationship with my boy and have always considered her a co-parent. She was the good cop, and I was the bad. But it was a balance that worked for our little family.

Keven and Therese

Then there was my mom. If Therese and Kev were close, he and his grandma were inseparable.

"Grandma, will you make me French toast?" She would.

"Can we go to the park, Grandma?" They could.

"Let's read, Grandma; here's 10 books." They did.

They had an extraordinary bond that made returning to work easy for me. I'd been hired part-time at a Christian ministry— one of the largest in the country. They had a local office, and I worked four hours a day until Keven was in elementary school; then I went full-time. My income, combined with the generous bonus I received, kept the bills paid. While I worked, Grandma walked Keven around her gorgeous yard and taught him about plants, flowers and trees. They'd go on excursions and walk the dogs. When he was about three, Keven went through a "dress-up" period, and I'd come home to find him in outfits he and my mom had put together—cowboy, pirate, Batman, ninja, fire-fighter and clown. Each St. Patrick's Day, she dyed their hair green for the day. They had inside jokes and secrets. When Keven was six, a typical evening went like this:

"I'm home!" The dogs ran to greet me. My mom and Keven snickered in the next room. They were huddled up on the couch looking guilty.

"What's so funny?" I asked suspiciously.

They barely suppressed their giggles with a devious shared secret. As I walked toward them, Keven leaped up and hugged me.

"Grandma let me mow the lawn today!" he exclaimed with delight.

I looked over at my mom, who was already defending her judgment to let him use the power lawnmower.

"I was right there the entire time, and he did a good job, didn't you, Kev?" She assured me.

Keven beamed with pride. "Grandma said you'd be really mad, but are you?"

Keven's first word was "lawnmower." He'd been bugging my mom to let him do this for years. How could I be mad when I saw his face? At 71 years old, she was more active than some people half her age. Her green thumb was legendary. The yard was her pride and joy.

"No, Kev, I'm not mad, because Grandma was with you. Just never try to do it yourself!"

Keven and Grandma

Keven's relationship with my mother reminded me of my own with my father. He was the best man I ever knew. He loved his family and worked 60-hour weeks to provide for us. He was a strict disciplinarian and a loving father. I have countless wonderful memories of him, my favorite being Sunday nights.

We would watch *The Ed Sullivan Show* as I sat on the floor in front of his recliner, leaning back against his legs. My handsome dad, whose eyes I'd inherited, wore his slippers and smoked a cigarette. My mom was busy putting my brother and sister to bed, so it was our special time.

When I was four, we watched The Beatles perform on the show, with all the crazy fans screaming. My young brain knew something was special about the guys on stage. They were cute, and the song they played sounded happy. The fans were entertaining but confusing to me. They seemed scared, like they were going to faint. But the excitement was contagious, and the next day my dad came home with their album. My lifelong love of rock-and-roll was born. When Dad was home, there was music playing in the house. It connected us.

My father passed away when I was 15, making my mother a widow and a single mom of three children. I stepped up as best as I could as a normal, selfish teenager. Looking back, I can see how I caused my mother way more stress than I offered her help. In my early teens, when my dad was fighting cancer, I acted out in ways she couldn't control. I was 13 and used the distraction of Dad's disease as an excuse to start relationships with boys that were beyond my emotional maturity. Attention from boys made me feel special—something I'd never experienced before. But needless to say, Mom didn't approve of me dating and having boyfriends so young.

I wanted my mom to be proud of me, but I disappointed her again and again by drinking, using drugs and staying out all night. She couldn't understand me, and in our family, we didn't talk about feelings, so it was a constant source of unresolved conflict.

I believe Keven healed my relationship with my mother. When he came along, she had a new purpose in life. Her greatest joy was her grandchildren, and now she had one living under her roof. She was 65 when he was born and still full of youthful energy. I think with all she had put up with from me when I was a teen, giving her Keven made up for it. I also like to think I made up for it later by taking care of her as she dealt with health issues and old age.

Keven's life might have been different if my dad was still here. In my room, there's a picture of my dad in his WWII uniform, taken when he was 17. He was a child and could only enroll by lying about his age. Next to Dad is Keven's senior picture. Their eyebrows, noses, the shape of their faces make them look like brothers. Maybe my dad could have been a positive male role model—or at least intimidate Keven into behaving. My siblings and I were well-behaved as kids because we knew Dad wouldn't allow us to get away with anything.

My dad and Kev would have had a lot to talk about. I love imagining them discussing cars and music and going target-shooting together. I still miss my dad. In fact, I missed him more when I became a mother. I can't help but wonder how things would have been different if he had lived.

David, my brother, was also a part of Keven's life. David was only 12 when our father died, Therese ten. One of our neighbors told David he was the "man of the house" from now on. It was too much to lay on his young, grieving shoulders, but he took it seriously.

From that day forward, he felt responsible for his mom and two sisters. He wasn't a man; he was just a kid. But David did his best to figure out how to live up to it. He was very protective of my mom, Therese and me. When Keven started using drugs and stealing from us, it created a lot of tension in the family because David saw what Keven put us through.

"Keven stole money from my wallet again!" my mother informed me. It was in the early days of Keven's drug use, and he hadn't figured out how to get his own money, so he stole from the three of us.

"Mom, I told you, you need to hide your purse or not keep cash in your wallet."

"This is my house; I am not hiding my purse!"

Eventually, she learned that no matter how much Keven loved her, his substance use was controlling his behavior. They both cried over it many times. I regularly heard him in her bedroom begging for forgiveness. She always gave it.

Watching her beloved grandson change from a sweet kid to a tormented substance user was agonizing. Mom never once stopped loving him or believing he would get through it. She went to family group meetings with me when he was in rehab. I took her to visit him in jail a few times, but it was too painful for her to see him in the bright orange jumpsuit and talk to him over a phone through the thick glass, so she stopped going.

I had brought my mother joy and finally made her proud of me. She watched me maneuver through the maze of Substance Use Disorder and recovery with her grandson. She respected the way I handled it. On the occasions that I did kick Keven out of the house, she'd beg me to let him come home. She couldn't stand the thought of him not getting home-cooked meals or having a bed to sleep in.

I spent a lot more time with my mom in her later years, and we became close for the first time in my life. She suffered through lymphoma and colon cancer and rallied to complete remission both times. On the last day of her life, she made dinner for Therese and Keven, then her famous Christmas cookies. Just after serving them, my mother suffered a stroke. She was 90 years old.

At the hospital, before Mom went into a coma, my sister, brother, Keven and I heard one more "I love you" as she attempted to lift her right arm to wave. I was suddenly a little girl again and wanted to run and jump in her arms and tell her how much I loved her. We had no way of knowing we'd never see her conscious again.

David, Therese and I took turns sitting by her bed in those last days. Her other grandchildren and her sisters also came to visit. Knowing she was going to pass, we talked to her and stroked her arm but got no response (except for a small smirk when we teased her about Alex Trebek being her boyfriend. She never missed *Jeopardy*).

Then Keven came to visit.

"Hi, Grandma, it's me, Keven." Before he could finish his sentence, her hand reached up for his. The room went silent. We were all stunned by her gesture. I had chills running down my arms as I watched him talk to her. "Here, Grandma, I'm giving you these because I know you like them." Keven always wore two stretchy bracelets with pictures of Catholic saints on tiles. He wasn't raised in the Catholic church, but my mom was, and so he called himself a Catholic to please her. Kev loved the symbolism, and he loved God. He put the bracelets on her thin, aged wrist. "It's going to be okay, Grandma; don't worry about anything. We'll take care of Chloe for you." We all sat, watching the two of them. Keven's voice stayed upbeat when he talked about taking care of my mom's dog, but I saw a tear slide down his cheek. Then, one last time, he said, "I love you, Grandma." She passed away the next morning with her three children at her side. A few days later, she was buried wearing his bracelets.

We only took care of Mom's beloved dog for 10 days. Without my mom, Chloe died of a broken heart.

CHAPTER 4
EARLY INKLINGS

> *Childhood trauma does not come in one single package.*
> ~Dr. Asa Don Brown, *The Effects of Childhood Trauma on Adult Perception and Worldview*

When he was five, Keven stood up in class holding a knife and said he was going to kill himself. I would never have known if a classmate's mom hadn't called.

"Hi Barbara, this is Sue, Katie's mom. I just wanted to ask how Keven is. Katie was concerned about him when she came home from school today."

"Keven? He's fine." What was she talking about? It sounded serious.

"Katie said he stood up in class with a knife and said he was going to kill himself. Didn't he tell you?" Sue sounded more concerned than judgmental (and, for this reason, was one of the few moms I felt comfortable around). Because I was one of the few single moms at the private Christian school—or maybe because we were on a scholarship—I never fit in with the other moms. I'd show up in my old Toyota Corolla and park among all the Mercedes and BMWs.

"Sue, I had no idea! I'll talk to him immediately. He was

probably just showing off. It wasn't a real knife—he got it from a souvenir shop during spring break." We talked for a few more minutes, but I was anxious to get off the phone and discuss it with Kev. What would make him do such a thing?

I found Keven playing with Legos on his bedroom floor, the room that used to be mine when I was a child. I had decorated these walls first with posters of animals, then later with rock stars when I became a teen: a larger-than-life-sized poster of Peter Frampton along with Jim Morrison, the Rolling Stones and Led Zeppelin. There had been crates of record albums organized alphabetically by band and the cherished stereo my father got me when I was 12. Incense, beads, tapestries—I always thought I was born too late because I was a '60s hippy girl at heart. Janis Joplin was one of my idols. Now my son was surrounded by Legos, action figures and stuffed animals. I had painted the walls light blue. Stepping carefully around his creations, I sat down across from him.

"Hey, honey, Katie's mom told me what happened today at school."

He looked up as if to ask, "Am I in trouble?" He was still wearing his school uniform—a red polo shirt and khaki shorts. He had a ring of chocolate milk around his mouth.

"You said you were going to kill yourself in class, so Katie told her mom she was worried about you. Why did you do that?"

It was a child's replica of a Swiss army knife. It wasn't sharp, but Keven certainly knew that it was totally inappropriate for school.

"I'm sorry, Mom! I didn't mean to upset Katie." His expression was sincere. Kev looked so innocent at that moment. He was smart and mature for his age, got along with other kids and seemed happy. Bringing his toy knife to school was out of character for him, particularly because he was always worried about getting in trouble with his teacher.

Kev couldn't give me an answer. He sat staring down at the pirate ship he was building.

"Do you see why this is wrong? You could get in trouble for bringing a knife to school, and you upset your classmates. Did you do it to get attention, or do you really want to kill yourself?"

"No. Neither of those. I don't know why I did it; it just happened."

Keven promised to apologize to Katie the next day. I couldn't get more out of him, so I dropped it. It felt like I'd gotten my point across, and he learned his lesson without punishment beyond me taking away the toy knife indefinitely.

I started to leave his room and stopped. "What did Miss Green say when this happened?" It suddenly occurred to me that she hadn't let me know.

"Nothing. She just told me to sit down," he replied.

Maybe I was overreacting. Maybe if I was there, it would have been obvious by the look on his face he was showing off or trying to shock the other kids. I could easily imagine that smirk he got when he was being mischievous.

At least 95 percent of me wasn't worried, but five percent wondered if Keven was thinking about killing himself. It seemed ridiculous to even contemplate—he was just a little kid! Why would a five-year-old bring a knife to school and threaten suicide? How did such a thought even enter his sweet young mind?

He had tons of attention at home, living with three women who loved him. Was it too much? Maybe I should stop spending so much time with him. My parents never spent time doing fun things with me when I was a kid, and I turned out okay. Or did I? A seed was planted in my head that day, but the rest of the school year went by uneventfully.

Keven loved Legos

That summer, when Kev turned six, he experienced a traumatic event. He had been invited to spend the day at the beach with a friend. I knew the mom, Debbie, and was happy Keven was invited. They were going to a familiar beach that he and I frequented in San Clemente. I thought of all the fun we had there and wished I didn't have to work so I could join them.

To get to the beach, you had to cross railroad tracks, but it was safe. People had been doing it for years, and there was always plenty of warning when a train was approaching and a clear view down the tracks in both directions.

When they arrived at the beach that morning, Keven noticed something odd: a man in a suit and tie was sitting on the curb in the parking lot drinking out of a bottle in a brown paper sack. Kev later told me that the man looked "out of place" because he should have been wearing swim trunks.

On the way home, the train was coming, so they stood and waited for it to pass. A few feet in front of them was the man in the suit. Right as the train approached, he stepped onto the tracks. Debbie pressed the boys' faces against her so they wouldn't see anything, but the image of the man walking in front of the oncoming train couldn't be erased.

Once again, I was caught off guard. "Barbara, it's Debbie.

How's Keven doing? I hope he isn't too upset." Her voice was nervous.

"Upset? About what?" I asked.

She told me the story of the man and the train. Like last time, I was anxious to get off the phone and find my son. This was huge! Why hadn't Keven mentioned it when I'd asked how the beach was? Debbie's son was so shaken that they'd spent the rest of the day watching movies to distract him.

I found Kev in his room, building with Legos again, this time working on a tall building with balconies and a Lego person standing in each one. It never ceased to impress me that he could make such elaborate creations at such an early age.

"Kev, how come you didn't tell me about the man and the train?" I asked gently. I picked up a few bricks and started to build a wall to go around his building.

"I don't know. I guess I forgot." He kept building without looking at me.

"Sweetheart, I know you saw something horrible. It's rare for something like that to happen, and he shouldn't have done it with kids around." I was starting to feel concerned because he was so casual about something so upsetting.

"It's okay, Mom. I didn't see anything bad. He must have had a bad life." I then tried to explain that sometimes when people are sad and hopeless, they feel like they can't go on.

Kev looked at me as if I were a child. "It's called suicide, Mom, and it wasn't a big deal. He was tired of living and wanted to go to Heaven." I kept trying different angles to get him to open up a bit to me.

"Did you feel scared? Were you upset when he stepped in front of the train?" Debbie had told me she didn't think the boys saw anything gruesome because it happened right after the train had passed them by. "No, Mom, it didn't bother me. I didn't see any body parts or guts."

Over the years, I brought it up occasionally to see if he was ready to say more, but always got the same answer: "It was no big deal." I've never been able to reconcile his reaction, why he wasn't traumatized or at least upset. It bothered me how unaffected he seemed to be.

Years later, when I was told he had PTSD and was asked over and over if anything traumatic had occurred in his childhood, I told each therapist about the train incident. He'd never brought it up to any of them. It drove me nuts to hear that my son had PTSD among his other issues without knowing for sure what caused it. He insisted he'd never been abused or molested and that nothing bad had ever happened to him.

Later in life, I believe many of the events he experienced due to substance use were traumatic, but as far as I knew, the train incident was the only traumatic occurrence in his young life. I will never know for sure how much it bothered him or if, as he said, it didn't bother him at all. But to me, that was more worrisome.

CHAPTER 5
DEPRESSION

> *A child's mental health is just as important as their physical health and deserves the same support. No one would feel embarrassed about seeking help for a child if they broke their arm—and we really should be equally ready to support a child with emotional difficulties.*
> ~Kate Middleton

Keven was eight years old when he faced his first big hurdle. After dusk on a hot August evening in 1998, someone knocked on the door. I opened it to find Keven with blood on his face; he was being held up by his best friend Ross and Ross's dad, Ron.

"What happened!" I hadn't bothered to look at his leg. I was focused on his bloody cheek.

Ron told me that Keven had been riding a go-ped and crashed into a wall at the school by our house. Then he pointed out Keven's leg. "You might want to have that checked out."

Keven's leg was swollen to twice its normal size! Panic filled me from the toes up. He'd never been seriously hurt before—this was a first, and it looked bad. Therese grabbed her keys, and I carried Keven to the car. Though he was much too heavy for me, I didn't notice. On the way to the hospital, I tried to keep Keven calm. I sat in the back seat with him and kept his leg supported and comfortable.

"It's going to be okay, Kev, I promise."

Over the years, I would use this simple phrase repeatedly. Keven's response would always be, "I know, Mom." How could I dare to promise something that I had no control over? Things weren't always okay: there were times when they were horrible. Eventually, we came to understand it was better to say, "No matter how awful things are, we will get through it together; we are a team, and we love each other."

Arriving at Mission Hospital's emergency room was the first of many hospital visits over the next 20 years. The orthopedic surgeon on call that night was one of the best in our area. Dr. Marandola looked like he'd stepped off the set of *General Hospital*. He was a handsome Italian with a New York accent. He told us Keven would need surgery first thing in the morning as his leg was seriously damaged and broken in three places. Seeing the X-ray of Keven's broken bones, I almost vomited. Those were my baby's bones!

Once settled in a hospital bed, Keven looked up at me and said, "Mom, I'm scared. I don't want them to cut my leg open." It was the first of many times I'd see his eyes filled with panic.

"I know, sweetheart, it's scary. But the good news is you have the best surgeon in Orange County, and he's going to fix your leg. You won't feel a thing." I could only hope that I was right.

They gave Keven some pain meds. His eyes were getting heavy. "Okay, Mom, I believe you." Fear crushed my chest: I was scared too. Knowing he was scared and in pain tore me up inside. He fell asleep quickly, and I sat holding his soft little hand for over an hour.

Later, when I settled in on the cushioned bench in Keven's hospital room, I could look out the window and see the stars shining in the night sky. I had a strong Christian faith at the time. The bright stars reminded me of the Bible verse that said, "He counts the stars and calls them all by name." God knew my son's name, and I prayed for the surgery to go perfectly and for Kev not to be scared. I would say a similar prayer 16 years later in the same hospital regarding the same leg when an infected abscess caused the surgeon to warn me that he may have to amputate.

The next morning at 5:30 am, my best friend, Kathy, unexpectedly walked into the room carrying two coffees. The light haloed behind her made her look like an angel, and the coffee confirmed it. I was so relieved to see her and to have someone to talk to. Later she, Therese, my mom and I sat in the waiting room during Kev's surgery. Some friends from church were also there to sit with us.

As I sat pale-faced in my own little world of worry, I heard the voices around me talking to each other. Occasionally, someone would ask how I was. If you say, "I'm fine," then people usually leave you alone. I wasn't close to being fine; I had never experienced such fear. The surgeon was concerned about the growth plates in Keven's leg, which meant that if the surgery didn't go as planned, he would have one shorter leg for the rest of his life.

It was nice to have friends there to support us, but since they all knew each other, they were talking and laughing, and it got on my nerves. Wasn't everyone else worried to death? Therese later told me she had never seen that look on my face before, but she would see it again many times in the future: the look of being consumed with worry for Keven. The doctor walked into the room smiling and reported that the surgery was difficult, but Keven's leg would continue to develop normally. The tension in my body just melted away; I cried in relief and thanked him profusely.

A month after the accident, Keven started third grade in a wheelchair. He wasn't allowed to put any weight on his leg. He had an external fixator that was wrapped up in a bandage, but you could see the four bolts sticking out that were holding his bones together. Eventually, he'd graduate to a cast and crutches, then a walking cast. I'd pull up to school and park in a handicapped spot, fighting the bulky rental wheelchair out of my trunk, then help him hop to it on one leg. We'd roll off to the playground, and kids would surround him.

"Can I push you, Keven?" asked Jacob.

"Then it's my turn," said another boy. I tried not to be nervous; he loved being the center of attention. I marveled at how opposite we were from each other at that age. I've always been nervous when I'm the center of attention, but Keven had no problem standing up in front of a room, speaking to a group or being surrounded by his peers in a social setting. Social anxiety made me appear aloof or uninterested (when in reality, I was usually on the verge of a panic attack).

The school didn't have an elevator, which I found odd. So, when the bell rang each morning, the vice principal would carry Keven upstairs to his classroom. He was supposed to carry him down and back up for recess and lunch as well, but after the first few weeks, the novelty wore off, and most of the kids stopped paying attention to him—and so did Mr. Bach. He stopped bringing Keven down for recess and lunch.

"Mom, no one wants to play with me anymore. Recess and lunch are my favorite parts of school, and now I have to sit in my classroom alone; it's boring. I'm being punished for having a broken leg."

I called the school and let them know Keven needed to get out in the fresh air with the other kids, at least for lunch break.

"Mr. Bach takes him down when he can, but he has meetings and can't always do it," the school secretary told me over the phone. Back then, I was not assertive enough. I wish I could reach back in time and handle things differently. I should have told the school it was their choice not to have an elevator and that they had better get him outside for both recess and lunch. But I didn't—I relented because I was worried I would risk our scholarship for the next year.

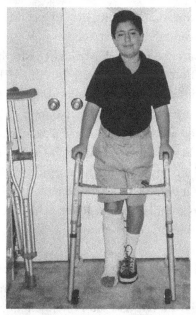

Keven with a Broken Leg

I convinced myself that it would be a life lesson for Keven, that he'd learn to cope with unpleasant situations. Now I understand that this was the beginning of trouble for my son. The feeling of being alone and isolated followed him throughout his life. He felt left out and less than his peers. He lost the comfortable, carefree disposition of a child. He was gaining weight from lack of activity, and the kids started picking on him and calling him names. My family saw it happening, and so did his teacher. I approached her on the playground one day after school when I was picking up Keven. Before I could say a word to her, she said to me, "Ms. Legere, Keven has stopped taking part in class and seems depressed. He's having a hard time with his assignments and rarely smiles like he used to."

My heart dropped at her words. I'd noticed Keven was struggling but had no idea it was this bad at school. At home, he still smiled and played, but due to the leg, Keven was limited in his activities.

"Have you considered taking him to a child psychiatrist? He may need medication," she continued.

Like most parents, I balked. My eight-year-old would not be put on medication. He would outgrow this. I believed it was directly related to his current circumstances: being alone at school and unable to walk. Her evaluation of him had to be wrong. But deep down, I knew my Keven was different. He occasionally told me how unhappy he was, long before the broken leg. I'd do my best to cheer him up. I blamed myself because I knew it bothered him not to have a father in the home. He would often complain about living with three women, even though he loved us all "to the moon and back and all around the universe."

I convinced myself that it was circumstantial, but what if it was more? Keven's unhappiness brought back memories of my childhood and how alone and sad I often felt, like no one had my back and no one really cared. My parents were great: they provided for all my needs, and I knew they loved me, but something felt like it was missing. There was no way I would allow my son to feel alone in the world. He had me, and I would do whatever I could to help him.

Before considering putting Keven on antidepressants, I took my doctor's advice and tried them for myself. I didn't want Keven taking something that I wasn't willing to take. My doctor had assessed me as being depressed years before I had Keven and had been gently suggesting medication ever since. He put me on Lexapro, and it helped me! It was true: there was a difference between depression caused by circumstances and a brain chemical malfunction. I was amazed at the difference—it lifted some dark clouds that had surrounded me my entire life, clouds that I assumed everyone had. I still got sad and upset on the meds if I had a reason to be. The difference was I wasn't depressed all the time for no reason at all.

When considering taking Keven to a psychiatrist, I didn't realize that he was also displaying signs of anxiety. Every morning before school, he would completely empty his back-pack to be sure he had everything he needed, then he'd put it all back and repeat the process two more times. No wonder it took him so long to get to school each day. He worried about some-thing going wrong—like forgetting his school supplies or being late to class—but he didn't elaborate on these details until years later.

Keven began seeing Dr. Kosins, a highly recommended and excellent child psychiatrist in our area. Kev had no problem opening up to the doctor. Once again, it amazed me how well he could articulate his thoughts and feelings at a young age. Keven was assigned to Michael, who was the only male therapist there. He loved Michael and talked about him a lot. Michael confirmed for me what I had already realized: Keven longed for a male role model and thought that he was less of a "man" because he didn't have what all his friends had—a father who lived in the home.

The meds helped Keven, but then he had a new challenge to face. Keven was being bullied by kids at school and one kid in particular who lived in our neighborhood. He had put on even more weight from taking the Lexapro they prescribed. I promised him he would outgrow his "baby fat" in a few years, but I knew that didn't lessen the pain of being called names and feeling left out. He begged me to change schools. There was a great elementary school right around the corner from our house where his best friends Ross and Andrew went. All three boys lived within six houses of each other, and he'd known Ross since they were both six years old. They were best friends for life. So, at the beginning of fourth grade, Keven started attending the public school by our house with his buddies.

Keven and Ross

Keven and Ross, 18th Birthday

Keven's depression and anxiety seemed a little better, and his smile appeared again. He didn't complain as much. He struggled with homework almost every night, and sometimes we'd both end up crying in frustration over math. Kev was smart; he tested off the charts in things like vocabulary and comprehension and got good grades in history. But math was difficult for both of us.

Keven had little interest in most of what he was taught in class, but when D.A.R.E. (Drug Abuse Resistance Education) came to his school, he was excited. He ran up to me when I arrived home from work that day and said, "Mom, I learned all about drugs today at school. They had a police officer come in and talk to us, and I got to see all kinds of stuff, even a needle they use for heroin. It was so cool!"

He was in fourth grade, and it alarmed me he found this so fascinating. Something that was intended to dissuade him from drug use excited him. We had our first talk about the danger of drugs and how they could ruin your life.

Keven's excitement should have set a parade of red flashing lights and sirens off in my head, but it didn't. I shrugged it off and filed it away as something to think about many years in the future, nothing to be concerned about now. Of course, now I wonder if I would have remained more diligent about his curiosity, could I have prevented him from trying heroin seven years later?

Other children continued teasing Keven for his weight and for his handwriting, which was almost illegible. Keven was diagnosed with dysgraphia, something I had never heard of before. This common disability presents as difficulty with handwriting related to issues with fine motor skills and sometimes vision problems. For kids, it's also linked to stress, frustration and anxiety. The stress can also manifest in other ways—such as poor performance in school or acting out. Keven was barely passing his classes.

Keven insisted the dysgraphia was a sign that he was dumb. I read to him straight from a medical website that it had no relation to intelligence or cognitive ability—many intelligent children struggle with dysgraphia and similar issues. This didn't convince him since he already felt like he didn't fit in. My heart hurt watching him go through this. I was constantly worried and felt powerless to help him. I believed in the power of prayer back then, but nothing changed. I did everything I could think of to boost Keven's self-esteem, but I was his mom. He needed to hear it from someone outside the family.

Therese paid for a special program that was supposed to help with dysgraphia. Keven went after school three days a week for a few months with no progress. They had him doing things like jumping on a trampoline while looking in a certain direction and playing with different materials to build hand and wrist strength. He was prescribed reading glasses. None of it helped much.

Keven told me he felt like he was a burden to our family when he overheard us talking about the cost. I assured him he was not a burden but the best thing that had ever happened in my life. His response—as it would be any time I tried to tell him he was special—was, "but you're my mom; it doesn't count when you say that."

The summer before sixth grade, Keven decided he wanted a new look. He wanted to appear tough so maybe he'd earn some respect from other kids. I allowed him to get his ears pierced. I, too, had enjoyed being unique and was the only girl at school who had triple-pierced ears on one side. It had become common for young men to have piercings, so I saw no harm in it. He also started styling his hair for the first time and wearing a leather bracelet and sometimes a necklace. Unfortunately, this gave the bullies another reason to tease him. As if the bullying from his peers wasn't enough, the biggest nemesis of sixth grade was Keven's teacher.

Starting the first day of class, Mrs. Underwood made sixth grade a miserable experience for Keven. She teased him in front of his classmates. She would use him as an example of what not to do. When he told me these things, I believed him. The few times I interacted with Keven's teacher, she was inappropriate and mean. On back-to-school night, when parents went to their child's classroom to meet the teacher, I was running a few minutes late. I am rarely late, so I was flustered and just stood there looking for an open seat. She said to me in front of all the other parents, "You must be Keven's mother. Your son threw up in my class on the first day of school. Sit at his desk over there." I didn't respond. I just turned bright red and sat down. I knew he'd thrown up—he'd been so nervous he had puked.

My second interaction with Mrs. Underwood caused me to go on a mission to get Keven moved to a classroom where he could learn without being bullied. When I was there for a parent-teacher conference, she said, "I bet sometimes you wish you wouldn't have had him." I was literally speechless because my mind was trying to determine if I heard her correctly or not. The school principal would not remove him from her class, so I went over her head to the superintendent's office. We had a meeting that included all three of them, and I brought along a friend of mine who was an elementary school teacher. But for whatever reason, they simply would not take him out from under this woman's obvious cruelty. It was one of the worst years of his young life. There was no one higher in the district to turn to. The school year was more than half over, so he had no choice but to live with it.

The summer between sixth and seventh grade, Keven grew several inches, and all his extra weight melted away. Contrary to most young adolescent experiences, Keven's junior high years were some of his best. The girls competed for his attention; the guys liked him. His grades were passing. I felt like we'd made it over the hurdle, and now life would get better for him. I couldn't have been more wrong.

CHAPTER 6
SINGLE-PARENT GUILT

> Single parents in particular may have trouble main-
> taining themselves as authority figures because of under-
> lying guilt; they feel a continuing sense that they have
> deprived the children of the second parent. So, they tend
> to give in to the children's requests even when unrea-
> sonable.
>
> ~Marge M. Kennedy and Janet Spencer King,
> The Single-Parent Family: Living Happily in a
> Changing World

Single-parent guilt plagued me. Kev complained about living with three women, but at the same time, he loved the attention, and he loved our family. I don't believe that a child needs two parents to have a healthy upbringing, but in Keven's case, he made it clear that he wished he had a father who lived with him. He made this known to me and to everyone else who would listen.

"I feel ripped off because I don't have a dad who spends time with me," I overheard him say to his buddies.

He'd ask me how he was supposed to learn to handle tools, throw a football, talk to girls and how to shave. He believed he was missing out on something that only dads could provide and that this made him less manly. I brought him into the world without a father, and I chose not to date when he was young, believing that he needed all my attention. Those felt like mistakes I had to live with and were a major source of guilt. Guilt. Lots of guilt.

Looking back, I should have dated more when Keven was young—I may have met a great guy who fulfilled that need in Kev's life. I simply had no interest at the time. Being a mom was all that mattered. I waited until Keven was older to date and felt I hit the jackpot when I met Jeff. He was a wonderful man— loving, honest and loyal. He was a single father with two children; their mother had died of cancer. When I was in my early 40s and Keven was 13, Jeff and I became engaged.

On a Sunday afternoon, Keven and I joined a family get-together with Jeff's family. It was the first time Keven met Jeff's children and the extended family. In his early teens, it was the last thing he wanted to do on a Sunday, but I'd insisted, knowing that once Jeff and I were married, this would be Kev's stepfamily.

Jeff's family was a melting pot of ethnicities and races. They were well educated, attractive and outgoing. As we entered their home, I saw that Keven got a few curious looks, but everyone welcomed him—or so I thought.

"Hi, I'm Keven," he said to Jeff's son, also 13 years old. Keven put his hand out for a shake, and Michael hesitated. Keven was wearing his usual ensemble: a band t-shirt and jeans along with his pierced ears, bracelets and other jewelry. He probably had on a hat as well with a brand name like Mossberg or Spyderco, popular brands among collectors of guns and knives.

When we walked outside to the large backyard, the kids dispersed to one end. Keven was talkative, and I could just imagine him telling them how much he hated school, loved knives, guns and cars—all while throwing in a few cuss words (his latest bad habit). The one thing these kids had in common was a strong Christian faith, but even that was different as we attended different churches. Keven and I went to a casual, non-denominational church where congregants showed up in jeans. The worship music had a rock and roll vibe—just our speed. Our pastor, Lyle, knew us and always made a point of saying hello to Keven after service, which meant the world to me. He also knew of my severe social anxiety and often invited me into conversations he was having with other members of the church. Jeff and his kids went to a large conservative church where they all sang in the choir and had never even met their pastor face to face.

From that day forward, there was always tension when the five of us got together. I struggled to see us ever working as a compatible family. I went back and forth between angrily wanting to explain that my son was "different" but a great kid and sadly wishing they would stop judging him. I eventually broke it off with Jeff for a lot of reasons, but this was the most important. While I strongly felt that it was my fault Keven didn't have a father or a stepfather who was there for him, I decided that this was not the right man for Keven or me.

I was thrilled each time a man would pay attention or spend time with Keven when he was young. It seemed like an answer to a prayer at the time, but in the long run, it did more harm than good because, in the end, he felt abandoned by each of them.

First, there was Chris, a firefighter we met when Keven was just three years old. He was at the local fire station's open house we attended during Kev's firefighter stage. Keven wore his firefighter uniform that day, complete with boots, hat and a yellow jacket. He was adorable. Chris took a liking to him and put him up in the driver's seat for a photo op (which later appeared in our community newspaper) and spent a long time talking to him. When it was time to go, Chris told us about another event that was coming up soon and invited us.

Keven counted the days until he got to see Chris again. When that Saturday morning arrived, he donned his firefighter uniform again, and we went to the local high school for the demonstration. Chris saw Keven and chose him to help with the fire hose. Keven got to pull the hose out as far as it went. He took this so seriously; his brow furrowed as he tugged and tugged. Toward the end, they had to help him a bit, and he got an enormous cheer from the crowd. When it was over and people were leaving, Chris asked Keven if he wanted a tour of the EMT truck. Once again, he spent a lot of time giving him one-on-one attention. When it was time to leave, Chris promised Keven that if he stopped by the station when he was working, he would put the ladder up and let Keven climb a few feet. Keven was ecstatic, and over the next few weeks, he was obsessed with seeing Chris again.

Keven and Chris

"Mom, when can we go see Chris? He wants to show me the ladder!" I knew that it wasn't the ladder he was looking forward to, it was the time with his new friend Chris. I called the fire station weekly, but Chris never had time for Keven again. I don't know whose heart was more broken, Keven's or mine. The last time I called Chris, I mentioned it wasn't a good idea to promise a young child something if you weren't able to fulfill the commitment. Keven was devastated and brought the incident up for years to come. That was his first time being let down, but it wouldn't be the last.

Several years after Chris, there was Jason, a young man I

worked with who met Keven a few times. He could see that Keven liked him, so he asked me if he could hang out with him a bit. I was so grateful and completely trusted Jason (who now has six children of his own). He took him to playgrounds and McDonalds; he roughhoused with him (something I never did). When Jason got married, he invited Keven to be a part of his wedding. He was too old to be a ring bearer and too young to be a groomsman, so he was the "train tender." Jason's bride had a beautiful long veil. Keven's job was to stand next to the best man, and every time the bride moved, he was tasked with moving her veil back into position. It was such a proud day for me. Not only did he look too cute for words in his tuxedo, but everyone also came up to me and told me how impressed they were that a six-year-old boy took his job so seriously. He added a special element to the ceremony. But that was the end of his relationship with Jason. Understandably, once married, Jason's focus was on his new life with his wife.

Ready for the Wedding

There was also Keven's junior high Sunday school teacher, whose day job was homicide detective for the Los Angeles Police Department—something quite cool in Keven's eyes. He meant well when he told Keven they would spend time together. They met for coffee a few times when Keven was in high school before he started having issues. I understood that the detective's life was super busy, so when the relationship came to an end, Kev also understood but felt disappointed. To our surprise, over the years, Keven and I saw him on several episodes of *Dateline* talking about murders he'd solved, and Kev would comment about how he wished they would have stayed in touch. At those times, I'd wonder if Keven would have thought twice about trying drugs if he had a cop for a friend.

Then there was an older gentleman Keven met at the hunting and fishing store we hung out at. Keven would sit on a stool while the older guy leaned on the counter and educated Keven on every type of knife, fishing rod and gun he had in the store. I would pretend to look at the merchandise, but I was really there for Keven's conversations. Unfortunately, the store closed after a few years. By then, Keven was older, maybe 12 or 13, and had come to understand that life includes disappointments. Once he no longer had access to this man who shared his wealth of knowledge about outdoorsmanship, Keven discovered the internet. He devoured information from the web and magazines on all things related to fishing, hunting and target sports like shooting and archery. But his primary passion was cars. I was blown away by his resourcefulness and knowledge—everyone was. I liked to call him a "walking automotive encyclopedia."

These men had no intention of hurting Keven. Unfortunately, his feelings of abandonment were compounded each time a new man came and went from his life. I did my best to bring positive male figures into Keven's life, but what he needed was his father. I knew that Jim loved Keven, but Keven only saw him twice a year—on his birthday and at Christmas. Jim wasn't capable of being more present in Keven's life, and I couldn't make up for that. The absence of his father was a hole in Keven's heart that no one else could fill. And I couldn't change Jim.

To ease my single-parent guilt, I bought Keven almost anything he wanted, thinking it would somehow make up for the lack of male attention he craved. I spoiled him. It's one of my biggest regrets. Instead of building character, I allowed him to feel entitled to whatever he wanted. It wasn't a matter of buying him toys so much (although I spent a fortune on Legos); it was paying for everything that he had an interest in and getting the best equipment "so it would last." He got to try fishing, surfing, skateboarding, archery, karate, snowboarding, target shooting, drones, paintball and too many other activities and pastimes to remember. The only thing I said no to was fencing because it was way too expensive.

At the time, I believed that if Keven could find something that he had a passion for and excelled in, he would have more confidence in himself and hopefully be less depressed. It didn't work. For me, it just produced more guilt and disappointment in myself. I sincerely believed I was doing the right thing by providing him with all these opportunities to try new things. On the positive side, I also spent a lot of one-on-one time with Keven, which I certainly don't regret at all. I have a catalog of special memories. Spending the day at the beach with our boogie boards was one of our favorite things ever. We stayed in the water for hours, waiting for the good waves to catch a ride to shore. We both loved how silly and happy these times were: the sun warming my back as I floated next to Kev, the droplets of water on my skin and the scent of the salty ocean air. Next to me, my child was laughing and smiling, the sparkling ocean a back-drop for his happiness. During those moments, all was well in my world. It was just my boy and me in a bubble of bliss.

Between the ages of five and eight, Keven would say that he was a shark, and I was a mermaid and that we were best friends. As a lazy wave approached, we'd yell, "Dud-hopper!" and glide over it. When a rideable wave was heading our way, we'd yell,

"See ya later," and try to catch it. One time when we were walking back to our chairs for a break, there was a squirrel kicked back in my chair eating a sandwich he'd taken from our lunch bag! He was holding it with both hands, just like a person would. He kept eating until we were only a few feet away before running to hide in the rocks. It was hysterical, and Keven loved squirrels from that day forward.

Fun at the Beach

When the boogie board days ended, I felt a deep sense of loss. All kids reach an age when hanging out with Mom is no longer the cool thing to do. The simple pleasure of floating in the ocean with the warm sun on our backs, laughing and talking and saying silly things that were just for us, was one of the best feelings I've ever had. I loved my little shark with every ounce of my being. Memories of Keven, carefree next to me in the ocean, are a treasured gift. I believe it's a good thing we can't see our futures. I wouldn't have been able to enjoy those times if I had known the darkness that was coming.

We eventually found a few things Keven excelled in— driving, archery and target/trap shooting. I taught him to drive when he was eight years old! In a canyon close to where we lived, there was a dead-end road that never had traffic. It was lined with large oak trees that created a canopy, hiding us from anyone who might drive by. On most Sunday afternoons, we'd head out there, blasting music through the open windows (switching between my music—Bruce Springsteen, Led

Zeppelin, The Doors and his music—Blink 182, Sublime and Eminem). Once on our special road, I would let him sit on my lap and steer the car. When he was too big to sit on my lap, I let him drive by himself up and down that road.

"Okay, Kev, just drive to the end of this road, and then we'll switch places, so I can turn the car around."

"Sure, Mom, whatever you say." He drove to the end of the road and did a perfect U-turn.

"Okay, honey, stay on the pavement and go really slow. Good, good. Now turn onto the dirt road—Damn it, Keven, *slow down!*"

Keven loved driving fast. I think he inherited his driving abilities from my father who had been an amateur race car driver. There we'd be in my white Nissan Altima, me just hoping we wouldn't get caught and Keven confident he'd be the next Jeff Gordon. We kept up our Sunday drives for years.

Once Keven was licensed to drive, he became an expert driver in every way, and drifting—in which the driver purposely oversteers and loses traction in the rear wheels while maintaining control of the car—was his specialty. He had a reputation among his peers for driving fast with skill. He'd take them out in the middle of the night to race through the streets. I was unaware of it at the time, but I later heard some wild tales from Keven's friends. He never got in an accident, and he only got one speeding ticket in all those years. If only I could have steered his life in a different direction. I never imagined that it would take such a drastic turn.

Keven was also an exceptional marksman. He excelled in archery and target shooting. When he was a teen, we set up our backyard with targets for his bows: recurve, compound and crossbow. It wasn't uncommon to find him standing in our front door with his bow pulled back, ready to shoot through the wide-open back door. He'd shoot the arrow straight through the house, typically making a perfect bullseye. There's still an arrow in the post of our front door that he put there a few years ago. I can't bear to get rid of it because it's a reminder of something he loved until the end.

We took up trap and target shooting, something I had watched my father do when I was a kid. Kev was a natural. Everyone around us at the indoor shooting range took notice of this 12-year-old boy who could hit a target dead center.

"Where did you learn to shoot, young man?" was a common question. Keven's reply was "YouTube," and it was true; he learned so much from watching videos. We'd also taken safety courses and a course in shooting, and Keven passed both with perfect scores. He taught me how to shoot, but I never did get a bullseye with a handgun, only a rifle.

Trap shooting was the best because it was an opportunity to hang out with the same group of older men each week, most of them in their late 50s and 60s. There was a private outdoor gun club in San Clemente that was open to the public on Saturdays. For a few years, we spent Saturday afternoons there doing trap shooting.

The range master went by the name "C," and he coached Keven whenever he had the chance.

"Where'd this kid come from?" I heard one guy ask C.

I proudly spoke up from the viewing bench, "That's my boy!" and he commended me for allowing him to pick up the sport. "You need to nurture your son's natural talent; he's one hell of a shot."

"That's why we're here every week!" I replied.

We saw most of the same shooters every week, and Keven was their unofficial mascot. I was so proud of my son—not just his ability but how mature he was and how he always thanked them for any advice they'd give, reaching out to shake their hand. In trap shooting, you aim at five clay "pigeons" from five different spots. When you say, "Pull!" the clay pigeons come flying out from a random direction. If you shoot all 25 pigeons, the whole event would stop so shooters could throw that victor's hat in the air, making it the new target. The first time Keven shot

25, the whole place was hooting and hollering. They threw Keven's hat up in the air, and he wore that hat filled with buckshot holes with pride. I will never forget the look of satisfaction on his face. Sadly, the gun club was closed down a few years later, but we kept shooting at the indoor range near our home. Shooting is an Olympic sport, and I have no doubt that if it weren't for drugs, Keven could have made it to that level.

Guilt has a grip on me these days, and I ruminate on all the things I did wrong. But I can't move on with my life after Keven's suicide if I allow myself to dwell on my mistakes. All parents make mistakes. I made some big ones. I do my best to convince myself that all my mistakes over the years were made in love—the overwhelming love I had for my son.

CHAPTER 7
SUBSTANCE USE HITS HOME

> *The worst part of anything self-destructive is that it is so intimate. You become so close with your addictions and illnesses that leaving them behind is like killing the part of yourself that taught you how to survive.*
>
> ~Lacey L.

"Damn it, where did all the spoons go?" I stirred my morning coffee with a fork and went out back to enjoy the early morning quiet. Sitting there, I tried to stay in denial for just long enough to finish my coffee, but I knew.

Other things were missing, too: ballpoint pens, aluminum foil and even the syringes I used on our dog for her daily insulin shots. I had to face the fact that after a brief time of sobriety, Keven was back to using heroin.

I finished my coffee and trudged up the stairs to his room. He wasn't there—he'd left in the middle of the night. This was never a good sign. I was so naïve back in the first few years, thinking Keven's drug use was a problem that could be fixed with the right solution. We would find the best approach to help him quit, and then he could carry on with his life. He would get an education, a job, a wife and then I would get my parental reward: grandchildren!

Standing in the doorway of Keven's room, my mind wandered back to the days when it was furnished with a crib and a rocking chair. I could remember the exact moment that love infiltrated every cell of my body as I looked down at my baby boy. It floored me. The feeling was new to me—like all parents, I didn't know this feeling existed. I'd experienced love before—giving and receiving—but this love was so pure and strong. I was afraid to ask other mothers if this feeling was normal because what if it wasn't for them? I never wanted to make anyone feel bad. I knew I was blessed to have this little guy put in my care. I would protect him and teach him and always be there for him. Loving, teaching and being there were easy. Even in his most unlovable moments, I unconditionally loved Keven every minute of his life—I still do. But protecting him? That is where I failed.

I first found out Keven was using heroin when he was 17 years old. Up until then, I knew he'd been smoking weed and drinking occasionally, but it never crossed my mind that he'd tried other drugs.

One night, Therese picked Keven up at a friend's house. He'd called and asked for a ride, thankfully recognizing that he was too high to drive. On the ride home that night, Therese could tell this was not a normal high from marijuana, and she managed to coax the truth from him. Keven had been experimenting with something much more dangerous than alcohol or weed. Despite his protestations, Therese told him, "You are going to tell your mom, or I will!"

Later that night, he and his girlfriend woke me, anxious to talk. I squinted up at Keven and the petite blond, wondering what couldn't wait till morning.

"Um, Mom, I have something to tell you," Keven said softly. Like any parent under these circumstances, I prepared myself to hear that Courtney was pregnant.

"Well, you know Jon, Kelly and Anthony? A few months ago, they were getting high on heroin, and Kelly talked me into trying it, and I've been using it ever since."

My middle-of-the-night logic wheels were stuck. *Heroin*? No one used heroin. That was something Vietnam veterans did when they got back from war, or musicians like Janis Joplin, Jimi Hendrix and Jim Morrison—not healthy high school kids who played sports and loved their families!

I knew that an early indication of drug trouble on the horizon is a change in social groups, but Keven's new friends, Jon and Kelly, were just like him: polite, nicely dressed and from loving homes. They were responsible—both had jobs and attended community college part-time. Anthony was a little rough around the edges, but I knew his story. He was living with his grandparents who had taken custody of him because his parents weren't fit to raise him. The idea that the three of them had been using heroin was absurd to me. The opiate epidemic hadn't surfaced in the media, so this news at my bedside was shocking.

Like most early substance users, Keven promised me he'd learned his lesson and wouldn't use again. Of course I believed him. Here he was confessing to me—being honest in the wee hours of the morning. Why would I think otherwise?

Then things started going missing around the house: cash, jewelry—anything that could be sold at a pawn shop quickly for a few dollars. Denial worked for a while until I realized it was a deceitful enemy that needed to be permanently kicked out of my mind. Since that first confession, Keven had never stopped using, and he was now in serious trouble.

We had a family meeting, and Keven admitted to my mom he'd been using heroin. I watched her face change from shock to anger. Like me, it was impossible for her to imagine her devoted, loving grandson involved with such a serious drug. Keven had only ever been in trouble twice but nothing that set off major warning bells.

The first time Keven got busted by the police, he was 15 years old. A large group of kids were smoking weed and drinking at the nearby park. We lived in Mission Viejo, California, a quiet suburban community. A resident had called and reported them, so when two patrol cars arrived, most of the kids ran off and got away. But not my boy. Not only was he one of five boys caught, but he was also the only one that got handcuffed and cited because he was mouthing off. This was my first "Ma'am, we have your son detained" phone call, and I learned that night that alcohol brought out the worst in Keven.

Then there was the call from his high school saying he was being detained by an Orange County Sheriff in the principal's office for being high in class. He was expelled from school at the beginning of his senior year. Things escalated quickly from there.

As soon as Keven hit 18, the calls came directly from him. Nothing prepares you for answering the phone at 3 am and hearing, "Mom, I'm in jail." But it became so normal that I set up an account with Global Tel Link (GTL—a service that handles incarcerated peoples' calls) and kept money in my account for both Keven and his friend Anthony. I can still hear the recorded voice because it became so familiar: "This is Global Tel Link. You are receiving a pre-paid call from (Keven!) an inmate at the (jail or prison name). If you would like to accept this call, please say or dial five now." As a haunting souvenir, I still get those calls from Keven and Anthony's friends who have my number.

Not long after our family meeting, Keven was arrested for possession. We were all in shock that our boy was in jail! Jail was for criminals! Because he was a first-time offender, Keven was offered the opportunity to go to a treatment program rather than serve time. Called "Recovery Court," this process included psychological screening and counseling, in-patient rehab and probation for three years which involved showing up at Recovery Court every two weeks. Once completed, the felony would be dismissed from Keven's record. He gladly took the deal.

Families were encouraged to attend court sessions, so I went every time. Recovery Court had its own building, and it was unlike any court experience I'd ever seen. It was located on Main Street in Santa Ana, connected to the probation office. Though constructed of drab, gray concrete on the outside, the inside of the court was beautiful, with wood walls and a comfortable, pleasant courtroom. Once court was in session, the judge pulled three names out of a hat. The three lucky winners would receive a gift card for food, music or coffee. Next, she would call each participant up individually and ask specific questions about how their program was going. In this positive and nurturing environment, we families all got to know each other well.

The first time I attended, Keven was in an orange jumpsuit in the glass "cage" because he had been waiting in jail for an opening at Phoenix House, a county-funded treatment center. When Judge Lindley spoke with him, he asked if he could wait for an available bed from home as he'd been in jail for four weeks already. She denied his request.

Later that morning, she called my name to approach the bench. Why me? She hadn't called up any of the other parents! I felt curious eyes staring as I walked up to the front of the room.

"Ms. Legere, I want you to understand why I am keeping your son in custody. I'm afraid that if I let Keven out of jail, he won't make it long enough for a county-funded bed to open for him. The level of heroin in his system when he was arrested was alarming; it was a lethal dose. He should have been dead. If your son's drug use continues at this level, chances are he won't make it."

I was stunned. I had no idea the severity of Keven's usage, and I didn't understand how he could have a lethal dose and still be alive. I later learned that he was a "slow metabolizer," one of the reasons Keven's tolerance was extremely high. He was only alive because his body wasn't processing the drugs fast enough.

The judge's ominous words in the courtroom were a cold glass of water thrown in my face. I was now fully awake and understood how serious Keven's drug use was. Every morning I would wake up wondering if he'd survive the day. At 18, Keven was one of the youngest people entering his rehab, and I couldn't have known that this help he so desperately needed was only the beginning of Keven's journey into a cycle of relapse. After 18 months in Recovery Court, Keven was terminated from the program because he was unable to supply "clean" drug tests consistently.

CHAPTER 8
REHAB—RELAPSE—
REHAB—REPEAT

> *You can get the monkey off your back, but the circus never leaves town.*
> ~Anne Lamott, *Grace (Eventually): Thoughts on Faith*

Keven's room was dark. He liked it that way, so we had painted it a deep shade of blue. He kept the curtains drawn, so I had to crawl across his bed to open them. The floor and bed were littered with empty Rockstar cans, a full ashtray of Marlboro Smooth butts, candy wrappers, dirty dishes, CDs, books and clothes. Gross. Even under these conditions, it didn't take me long to find a black metal box filled with paraphernalia, including used syringes and burned spoons. I had learned over the years that Keven's heroin was always hidden better, usually in a very creative way. Every time he went to rehab, he would ask me to get everything out of his room and told me where to look—under pieces of carpet that had been cut away from the wall, in the model cars he kept on the top shelves, behind the plastic plate of an electric outlet or under the bathroom sink.

My stomach turned as I sat holding the metal box and looking at all the household items that he had repurposed to shoot or smoke heroin: the bottom of soda cans, aluminum foil with black burned lines, straws, lighters and the tips from cotton swabs and shoelaces. When you're the parent of a substance user, your life evolves in such a way that "normal" is a forever shifting goal post. You don't ever imagine that you might become familiar with a drug kit or secret hiding places for packets of heroin.

Sitting cross-legged on Keven's bed with the box in my lap, I felt nauseated, my head pounding. I didn't have the energy left to cry. Should I offer rehab again? He'd already been to at least ten. It was hard to keep track because there were so many. I knew that forcing him to go never worked; it had to be his idea.

Paraphernalia in a Black Metal Box

Keven's first experience at rehab, he was 18—a 90-day stay at the Phoenix House in Santa Ana. He did well for a while after release, but after a few months, he relapsed. Then between the ages of 19 and 21, there was Cornerstone, Unidos, Twin Town and 10 Acre Ranch Riverside, where he completed anywhere from 30 to 120 days. Each time he would be sober for a short period, then relapse again. In 2011, he went to Woodglen in Fullerton, left on his second night and was almost immediately arrested. There were countless other facilities—Above It All,

Sunshine Ranch, Hollywood House, Pat Moore Foundation, Solid Landing, Nancy Clark, Chapman House and Gerry House. From his first rehab at 18 to his last when he was almost 30, Keven went to 15 different drug treatment centers, six sober living facilities and 11 detox centers. Whether he completed two, 14, 30, 90 or 120 days of treatment, Keven would get kicked out for using, or he would relapse upon leaving.

On and on it went. He would come home determined, go to meetings and do well for a few months, weeks or days. Then it was back to using again. Sometimes, instead of coming home, he'd go to a sober living or do an Intensive Outpatient Program (IOP). There was no difference. Keven thought about using 24/7. He dreamed about it. Keven grew more and more disappointed in himself for not being able to stay sober. He was losing hope. I was losing Keven.

Rehab typically costs from $3-5,000 for seven to 10 days at detox. I paid $10,000 once for a 30-day rehab ranch and felt like I was getting a deal. My mom and Therese also helped over the years with the expenses. I know my mom shelled out over $11,000 once in the beginning of our rehab experience for what his insurance didn't cover. We thought that paying for the best 90-day facility around would mean he'd come out "fixed." The total cost was $50,000.

But expensive facilities aren't always the answer. Unidos was only $400 a week and Keven stayed there for a full 120 days. It was a run-down environment with horrible food, bed bugs and broken windows. But the staff genuinely cared. I think it also helped that it was all-male—co-ed could be distracting for everyone.

Keven was fortunate to get a few scholarships along the way, and I will be forever grateful for those that gave him that opportunity. His sobriety was always short-lived, no matter what type of treatment he received. One time I thought he had almost nine months of sobriety but then learned that it was actually four: Keven had found a way to function by using just enough to not get sick. I couldn't tell he was using. He went to work every day and performed well.

Each time Kev came to me and said, "Mom, I need help. I want to go to rehab," I would feel like I was headed to battle. The process of making call after call was stressful, exhausting and infuriating. There were times I found myself begging for help. Keven was in such bad shape, and I needed to seize the moment before he changed his mind. If he wanted help on a Monday and there wasn't an opening until Friday, the window of opportunity would close.

Finding treatment that's effective, affordable and has immediate openings is grueling. You know it's out there somewhere, but it takes a lot of work and determination to find it.

From what I witnessed, most drug treatment centers are run in similar ways. There were discussion groups, one-on-one counseling and required attendance of AA and/or NA meetings. The majority of the facilities relied on the 12 steps of Alcoholics Anonymous as the guidelines for recovery. Everyone was expected to do certain chores in an effort to create accountability and to challenge residents to meet responsibilities. Most residential treatment programs were in homes, so there was cooking, cleaning and laundry to do. Some were co-ed, but usually, men and women lived in separate houses. Rehab worked for some people but not all. Almost every substance user I know attended more than one rehab.

Typically, Keven and I would make a list, divide it and both make calls. We'd start early in the morning, reaching out to facilities that we were familiar with, then move on to any new resources we'd found. I would contact everyone I could think of who might know of a new place to try. We'd take notes on every conversation, and most calls required us to call back again later or to wait for a callback.

"Hello, do you have any openings?" Keven and I would always start hopeful.

Then we'd answer their litany of questions:

Are you calling for yourself or someone else?

What kind of insurance do you have?

What drugs are you currently using?

When did you first start using drugs?

Have you been to rehab before?

What motivated you to seek treatment now?

What other substances do you use?

How much do you use on a typical day?

How has drug dependency impacted your life?

What is your medical history?

What is your mental health history?

Are you on any medications?

What is your employment history?

What is your financial situation?

What are your family and home life like?

When we finally heard back from one of the facilities, Keven would answer all of the questions he could, but if he was too high, I'd put the call on speaker and keep him on track. I recall biting my tongue because it would have been so much easier for me to take the phone and answer quickly, but it was important for him to know he was capable.

If we found a place that said "sliding scale" or "we turn no one away for financial reasons," we learned that in every case, it was a lie. This was a lure to get you to call so they could convince you to commit to paying a certain amount. I'm not saying that true sliding-scale rehabs don't exist; I'm saying that in all those years, I *never found one that was legitimate.* I don't know how they get away with making this claim, but they do.

Once the treatment facility was secured, the next challenge was getting Keven ready to physically walk out the door and get into the car. Even if he was packed, he would use the whole time leading up to our departure. Some places provided transportation, which always made it easier for me.

Heroin users go to rehab high. This is just a fact that I had to accept. They expected people to show up high, and it gave the staff a way to monitor when Keven's urine should show up as "clean." The only way for Keven to step foot into a treatment facility was to get high first. I admit to paying for heroin on a few occasions, just so he'd walk through the doors.

Sometimes I'd get him out of the car and drive off as fast as possible before he could change his mind. Most times, I went in until he was admitted. Sitting in the lobby, I'd look around at other parents, some crying and distraught, others like me—tired of the same old routine but never giving up.

I was helpless and lost and didn't know how to help him. No combination of rehab, recovery program, sober living facility or IOP was working. No one I talked to could offer alternatives—other than kicking Keven out of the house. That hadn't worked either. He ended up using in more dangerous ways and developed hepatitis C from using dirty needles. Keven may have had HIV; we never knew for sure because his test results came back both positive and negative. My son was getting sicker and sicker and his life more and more in danger, and I was out of answers.

Recovery isn't for people who need it; it's for people who want it. You can't make someone go to rehab, and even if they go willingly, there are no guarantees. If success was based on a desire to do well, a lot more people would still be here today.

Crossing the hallway, I went into my own bright and cheery bedroom—my sanctuary—and sat at my desk. Journaling was something I'd done most of my life, and that day I wrote, "What could I have done differently?" I filled the page through tear-blurred vision. I was a failure. I had failed Keven. Then, at the end of the page, I wrote, "Stop this right now! You are a good mom, and you're doing your best; none of these things caused Keven to start using drugs!" I wanted to be right. I knew logically that parents aren't to blame for their child's substance use. There's no way to know whether Substance Use Disorder will take hold of them until they have their first or second drink or try their first drug. In many cases, one use of heroin is all it takes for someone to get addicted.

The three most dangerous words a parent can say are "not my kid." A lot of parents assume that their child is smart enough and educated enough to say no that first time. We teach them the dangers of drugs from the time they are young. Yet looking back, many of us heard the same things from our parents and went ahead and experimented with the drugs of our day—maybe marijuana, cocaine or pills—but Keven was born in 1990, and heroin was the street drug of his generation.

With heroin, a first-time user's curiosity almost always outweighs any warnings they were given about potentially ruining their life or even dying. I have met only two people who tried heroin and were able to use it sporadically—the way many of us can enjoy a drink now and then and not have it take control of our lives. I survived my years of drinking and using drugs because I didn't have the disease of Substance Use Disorder. I was able to stop when I wanted to, and it was never a struggle.

An hour went by while I journaled, contemplating my role in Keven's most recent relapse. It angered me that he'd used again, but I'd been around this block enough times to understand that relapse is part of recovery. Getting angry just made things worse for both of us. I knew he would be disappointed in himself. Nothing compares to the pain of watching your child suffer through Substance Use Disorder. It feels like little sharp knives stabbing you over and over. You have no choice but to live with the pain.

When Keven came home, I could tell that he was in a great mood. Keven was wearing his purple plaid, button-down shirt with the vest from his gray suit, a pair of gray pants and his Bruno Maglio loafers that I'd gotten him for $40 at a thrift shop. He looked put-together and handsome. Another hard truth parents learn about the different types of drug use is that heroin doesn't mess with your looks like meth does. Keven was actively using, but he looked healthy. Those who were around him recognized his heavy-lidded eyes and the dark stains and sticky black tar around his fingertips that left black smudges all over the house. But to the general public, he looked fine most of the time.

I returned to his room and sat with the black box on my lap. When Keven came upstairs, his smile faded. "What's going on, Mom? You can't just walk in here and invade my privacy."

I reminded him that because of his drug use, he had lost the privilege of privacy. The confrontation eventually turned to tears as he walked me through his latest relapse. We had the familiar conversation. He was sorry. He was doing his best. He wanted to stop. He promised it would never happen again. Like always, I wanted to believe him. But I was hopeless. We were out of options and had nothing new to try.

Keven Enjoying Sobriety at a Drug Treatment Program

CHAPTER 9
A SECOND SON

Wounded children have a rage, a sense of failed justice that burns in their souls. What do they do with that rage? Since they would never harm another, they turn that rage inward. They become the target of their own rage. They repeat in their thoughts the same harmful words that were spoken to them. They must lash out, but the only ones weak enough to attack are themselves.

~Woody Haiken

Keven was 16 when I started hearing about Anthony, and everything I heard made me nervous. He had a reputation as someone you didn't want to get in a fight with because he would always win. Anthony had already spent time in juvenile detention as well as jail for drug possession. Anthony was 20 years old. Kev begged me to give him a chance.

"Mom, if you knew him, you'd like him." Kev was right: Anthony stole my heart. He was just a kid longing for a mother because his had died when he was just 14. Her drug of choice was meth. Although Anthony's mother survived a meth lab explosion that burned her face, arms and hands, she continued to use. She died when her motorcycle hit the back of a truck, leaving Anthony and his younger brother, Timmy, behind to be raised by their dad—a drug user who was abusive to his wife and two sons. Anthony's dad spent his days in and out of prison. Only four years old, Anthony tried to protect his little brother and mom from his violent father: "When I could tell he was going to beat on us, I'd grab Timmy and climb up this tree and hide."

When Anthony was only 15, his father stole a car. After a police chase, his father abandoned the car and ran. He left Anthony behind, telling him the cops wouldn't bust him since he was a kid. The cops did arrest Anthony, and he was sent to a juvenile detention facility. After that, he was constantly in and out of jail or prison.

Anthony was well-known by the local police and they often stopped him whenever they saw him. He was once standing outside of a Del Taco drinking a soda when they searched him. Because Anthony was on parole, the police hauled him in for possession of marijuana.

Because of this, Anthony developed the instinct to run whenever he was pulled over or stopped. He couldn't control it—even if he had nothing to hide, he'd take off. Running from the cops is never a good thing, so he was tased a few times and attacked by K-9s at least twice. Anthony loved dogs, so even though he had bruises and bite marks from the incident, being attacked by dogs hurt him more emotionally than physically.

Although he had a reputation as a tough guy, the Anthony I knew and loved was a sad, scared little boy. All he desired was to feel loved, safe and wanted. He played guitar, sang, wrote songs and was an incredibly talented artist. He made money as a tattoo artist. Anthony's grandparents took good care of him and his brother for most of their youth—providing love and all the experiences of a "normal" childhood. The boys loved their grandparents, but nothing could make up for the loss of their mom and the trauma from their father.

Anthony was extremely popular in prison. He'd make up

songs and sing on request because he knew the lyrics to a lot of contemporary music. He'd create drawings for the incarcerated and the guards. One time when Anthony called me from jail, I could hear a bunch of guys begging him to sing his new song. I listened from the phone and heard the cheering and applause afterward.

Because Anthony and I wrote to each other every few days when he was in jail, a lot of his "cellies" got to know me, too. It's not uncommon to read letters out loud to each other. Because of this, I have a list of people with criminal histories who "have my back." Most of them have turned their lives around and keep in touch with me on social media.

Anthony used me as his emergency contact. Several times I received calls from hospitals around Orange County, letting me know he had overdosed or had been hurt. On one occasion, I sat next to him for a few days as he lay in a coma hooked up to life support. The doctor told me it was 50/50, Anthony might or might not live, and if he did, he could have brain damage. I felt like I was Anthony's mother in those long hours alone with him in that dark ICU room. I spoke with him and stroked his arms, surprised that his skin was so soft. Having just been released from jail, Anthony entered a sober living home and had used drugs the first night there. Since he hadn't used in a while, he miscalculated his dose, and they had to call 911. On the third day of life support, Anthony started coughing, and blood filled the tubing coming from his throat. I screamed for the nurse, horrified. She said not to worry—it was a good sign that he was breathing on his own again.

Anthony was surprised to see me when he woke up. Through his tears, he said, "You really do love me, Mom." Though he always introduced me as his mom, I had mixed feelings because it felt like a dishonor to his real mom. But I know I would want someone to mother my son if he lost me, so I wore Anthony's label as an honor.

On another occasion, I went to visit Anthony in the hospital when he had a broken cheekbone. I visited him every day he was there while they treated an infected abscess on his arm. One afternoon I showed up to take him home, and his bed was empty. The nurse told me Anthony had left AMA (Against Medical Advice) and had tried to sneak out with an IV in his hand. This tactic was an intravenous drug-users dream: a port to use instead of having to find a vein!

As I was leaving the hospital, Anthony called. He was not far away. I found him sitting on a wall near the hospital, wrapped up in a hospital blanket. I took him to my house.

"Mom, I fucked up again. I'm sorry. I had a friend meet me here and bring me some dope. I don't know how much more I can take this. I just want to die sometimes."

"Let's get you home. You can take a hot shower, and I'll make you something to eat. Right now, just be kind to yourself; don't beat yourself up. You'll get to the other side, I promise."

At my house, Anthony took a hot shower, but when I realized that the water had been turned off for at least 20 minutes, I knocked on the door. My heart clenched up when there was no answer.

I pushed the door open to find him passed out on the bathroom floor with my blow dryer in his hand turned on high. I could see that he was breathing, so I reached down to help him up.

"Hey, buddy, let's get you off the floor. You can take a nap in my bed."

"Okay, thank you." He was crying. I walked him to the bed and tucked him in like a child. I leaned over and kissed his cheek and stroked his forehead. My heart ached, knowing how painful life was for Anthony. He felt like he didn't belong anywhere, and he'd gotten himself into a lot of serious legal trouble. He wanted some normalcy, a permanent place to live, but I couldn't have him and Keven in the same house—it would be a disaster.

Anthony and Keven, The Early Years

Anthony

Over the years, my relationship with Anthony became a mirror of my relationship with Keven. I was supportive and encouraging of him but also got angry and frustrated with his choices. I drove Anthony places, got him into some rehabs and loved him with all my heart. My mother and sister loved him too. He was part of the family and often spent holidays at our home.

One night, Anthony called me, crying, saying he felt all alone in the world. I was in bed but got up and pulled on a jacket and jeans and drove to the address he had given me. I stopped on my way to buy him a pack of Camel Crush cigarettes, his favorite brand, something small to cheer him up. We stood under the black sky near the apartment where Anthony was crashing.

"I don't think I can last here much longer; life hurts too much," he said.

I had my arm around him as he said those words, and we were both gazing upward. Suddenly a shooting star flashed across the sky! I'd never seen one that lasted so long and seemed so close to earth. He was ecstatic, shouting, "That's my mom; that's her right there! A sign from my mom has always been a shooting star!" He cried with joy.

At 5 pm on September 7, 2015, my phone rang. It was Donna, Anthony's grandmother.

"Barbara, can you come over here right now?" Her voice was flat.

Less than 10 minutes later, I arrived to find their front door open. I knew as soon as I saw Donna that Anthony was dead.

"Anthony's gone. He died in Vegas—"

We held each other tight, both sobbing. The circumstances of Anthony's death were sketchy. It was ruled an accidental overdose but could have been prevented if the woman he was with had called 911. After emergency responders found Anthony, they called a homicide detective to the scene, and later, the lead homicide detective of Clark County called me and asked if I had any reason to believe there was foul play. Rumors had been swarming for months about how Anthony had made a deal with a local police agency that resulted in one of the prominent drug dealers in our area being sent to prison.

Was it a setup? Did this woman intentionally let Anthony overdose? She left him unconscious in the rental car and went up to their room. There was a hospital directly across the street, and an eyewitness heard her say she knew he was dying and didn't know what to do.

Anthony was found the next day in the car at around 11:30 am. The coroner would not allow us to see Anthony due to advanced decomposition from being in the extreme heat of the Las Vegas sun.

Keven, who was in prison at the time, was convinced that the drug dealer had a hit out on Anthony. I told the homicide detective what I knew, and he filed a report. A few days later, he got back to me and said they had no physical evidence, that it would be all hearsay and unlikely to be accepted by the district attorney's office. I agreed to let it drop. It didn't matter. Anthony was gone.

I gave the eulogy at Anthony's memorial service. It was a small gathering held at his mother's gravesite; his ashes were buried on top of her, and Donna generously gave me some to keep. Since Kev was in prison at the time, he couldn't attend, but he wrote a heartfelt letter, and I read it as part of the eulogy.

Losing Anthony left a huge hole in my heart. The grief was so intense and completely different from losing a parent, close friend or one of my other relatives. I felt alone because while Anthony was like a son to me, he wasn't actually my son. I worried that others thought I was exaggerating my loss. But I was mourning the loss of an incredible young man who was an important part of my life.

They're rare, but when I am blessed to see a shooting star, my entire body feels electrified—a cosmic connection with the son of my heart. I'd like to think that his mother, Karen, speaks to me through them along with Anthony, saying, "Thank you for watching over my boy till we were together again."

CHAPTER 10
RIDE-ALONG MOM

> *Nothing can compare to the chaos and turmoil of addiction. Feeding the beast is a full-time job and the constant desperation to avoid withdrawals never lets up. If someone you love is struggling with addiction, you'll need to have a basic understanding of the disease.*
>
> *~Nikki Seay, A Walk in My Shoes: One Day in the Life of an Addict*

E arly on in our struggles with Substance Use Disorder, I learned that what Keven needed most from me was understanding of what he was going through. I needed to empathize rather than criticize. Before I grasped what was really going on with Keven's drug use, we argued a lot, sometimes even screaming at each other. More than once, he yelled, "I hate you, Mom!" and I returned with, "I hate you too!" Even though we didn't mean the words we shouted at one another, hearing them was sickening.

I needed to learn about the cycle of using, recovery and relapse from the people who really knew what it was like, so I talked to the experts, Keven, Anthony and their friends.

The first time Kev tried to explain what it felt like to be in the evil grip of heroin, he knew I sincerely wanted to understand. He trusted me enough to be totally honest.

"Mom, it's not a choice. I have to use every day to feel normal. When I first started using, it was like I magically felt good. All my anxiety, fears, and paranoia were gone. It was the best feeling in the world—like everything was perfect and nothing bad could happen to me. It was the answer to all of my problems."

He lit a cigarette and continued: "After using for a while, you build up a tolerance, so you need more to feel good. That means you have to find more money to buy larger amounts. Every day starts the same for me. I wake up and wonder how I'm going to get money to pick up today? Sometimes I steal things that I can sell. Sometimes I find my connect a new client, and he will then thank me by giving me some for free. You don't even want to know some of the ways Anthony and I get money; you really don't." Listening to these details was torture, but I knew it was my only way to understand Keven. And if I could understand him, maybe I could help him.

"But that's not the worst part." He paced as he talked, always up and moving. He had a knife in his hand, flicking the blade out over and over. It was one from his treasured collection that he eventually sold for drugs.

"The worst part is I can't even get high enough anymore. Now I need to use just to stay *well*. If I don't use it every day, I go into withdrawals and feel like shit. You've seen me detox. You know how bad it is."

The first time Keven tried to detox at home, we went to a Substance Use Disorder specialist. He prescribed medications to address each of the detox symptoms to help get Keven through the next few days. I watched him experience sweats and chills, all-over body aches, vomiting, insomnia, aching bones and headaches. His body twitched with restlessness, which prevented him from sleeping. He was weak and pale, tossing and turning in bed, alternately soaking the sheets with sweat and then shivering under a pile of blankets. Keven said it was like the worst flu you could imagine on steroids.

During this time, I was unemployed for 18 months. My car became a safe place for Kev and his friends to talk, so I jumped on any chance to give them rides. His friends often needed rides to probation, parole, court dates or doctor appointments. I loved spending time with them and was usually available. All these kids reminded me of Keven and Anthony, and they needed all the encouragement and empathy they could get. They knew they could always call me. I was their ride-along mom.

When I would get one of those calls for help, Keven or Anthony came along to protect me from any sketchy circumstances if they were available. We'd take off in the middle of the night to rescue someone who was in trouble, paranoid or who had been ditched by friends and had no way home. Naturally, my friends thought I was crazy and stupid. I could only hope that someone would be there for Keven in the same situation. Every homeless kid I see is a son or daughter. They all need encouragement and love.

Out of all of Keven and Anthony's friends, Taylor was my favorite. I was his weekly ride to his probation appointment, and every time I picked Taylor up from the big yellow sober living house, he put a smile on my face.

Taylor was bigger than life, taking up more than his share of space with positive energy. He was a good-looking kid, tall like Keven with broad shoulders and long dark hair that he was constantly pushing out of his bright blue eyes.

One morning, he was dressed in his usual skinny jeans, a heavy metal band t-shirt, Converse All-Stars and a leather bomber jacket. He was beaming as he jumped in the passenger seat.

"Hey Mama Bear!" he greeted me. He never called me by my name—sometimes it was Barbie Doll, or Keven's mom or Rocker Chick. He could call me whatever he wanted. Being around him made me feel happy.

Taylor had come so far since I first met him at Phoenix House. On a family visiting night, I noticed him standing in a hallway leaning against the wall with his arms crossed in front of his chest. He was pouting like a little kid. As I passed by, I heard him say to his parents, "I want to go home!" I chuckled to myself because under all his tough, extroverted, over-the-top personality, he was just a kid. He and Keven both survived their first sober 90 days there, satisfying their first court order.

"So, Blondie, what's it gonna be today? I know you like the more mellow stuff, so I brought Metallica and Megadeath," Taylor said, sliding a CD into the player. He was deep into heavy metal and death metal bands and was a guitar player for his own band, Excised. On mornings like this, it was hard not to feel optimistic.

Driving down the freeway toward Santa Ana, Taylor told me his good news. "Dude! Check this out! I finished my classes! My parents are letting me move back home!" I saw the pride in his eyes and congratulated him on this enormous accomplishment. I'd been in family groups with Taylor's parents, and it was obvious how much they loved their oldest son. Taylor had three younger siblings who idolized him. They were thrilled to have their real brother back after his years of doing heroin and being in trouble with the law. Everyone was so proud of him for going back to Cal State Fullerton to finish his degree. His future looked promising.

I sat in the car and read a book while Taylor was visiting his probation officer. On the drive home, I stopped and got him his favorite meal at Wendy's to celebrate his good news. As I pulled up in front of the big yellow house and before Taylor jumped out of the car, he said, "I probably won't need as many rides from now on. My mom's gonna let me use her car. But don't worry—there's no way you can get rid of me! See ya later, Kev's mommy."

Taylor hugged me and jumped out of the car. I smiled and waved as I drove off, feeling disappointed that he no longer needed rides but thrilled at the reason for it. I'd miss these drives a lot. It was the last time I ever saw Taylor. About a year later, I got the call.

Taylor

In the months following that last drop-off, Taylor kept in touch with calls and texts, then it was letters from jail. His sobriety ended when his ex-girlfriend was killed in a car accident. I'd been so sure Taylor was done with drugs, but similar to cancer, Substance Use Disorder can go into remission, then take over someone's life again. With heroin, the possibility of picking up again never ends. I wish there was chemo and radiation treatment to rid someone of the desire to get high the way it can kill cancer cells.

The risk of using opiates again after a long period of sobriety is death. The tolerance to the drug is gone, so if you use too much, it can stop your heart. A sudden death following a surprise relapse is exceptionally difficult for family and friends because it comes out of nowhere.

Taylor was found by his mother on Christmas morning after

an accidental overdose. Anthony, Keven and I mourned together and drove around listening to a CD of Taylor's band, crying and laughing as we shared memories. Taylor was unforgettable, and his face and voice are loud and clear in my head, as if he were sitting right next to me.

Gilberto, a former gang member, was in his late 20s and a father of three. He was a house painter by trade but had a terrible fall on the job. His Substance Use Disorder, like so many, began with prescription opiates for pain. He switched to heroin because it was so much less expensive and easier to get. Gilberto worked his 90 days with Keven in sober living, and no one will ever know why he went back to using heroin. He was found in a parking lot, behind the wheel of his car, with the syringe still in his arm.

Keven had gotten close to Gilberto and his large Hispanic family. After visiting Gilberto at his home the first time, Keven was so touched by his community; Gilberto's mom, sisters, his wife and three kids all lived together in a huge apartment complex with a courtyard in the middle. Gilberto and his family set up tables outside their door next to their neighbors with more food than Keven had ever seen. He walked around the court-yard, helping himself like he was at a buffet in Vegas, with little kids of all ages running around laughing and playing.

"We all sat at tables in the courtyard. A bunch of the little kids really liked me and wanted to sit by me when we were eating. I teased them, and they loved it. I can't wait to go again next week."

Keven became a regular at their feast nights and got to know Gilberto's family well. We also loved having Gilberto over to our home, and Keven's grandmother doted on him, pushing Hawaiian pork chops and homemade apple pies. It was as if our families were competing for their happiness by filling their bellies.

Because Gilberto was a former gang member, not everyone had pleasant things to say at his funeral when the reverend opened the service for shares. About midway through, to my surprise, Keven approached the podium. He, Taylor and I felt like trespassers at this funeral, but our love for Gilberto was pure. My heart was pounding because I was nervous for Keven, but he spoke with confidence. There was no way Keven was staying quiet when he heard people up there dissing his "homie."

"I've heard a lot of negative things about my friend today," Keven said calmly. His voice was steady and kind. He described Gilberto as he saw him: devoted to family and friends, honest, someone who tried extremely hard to stop using drugs. It was quiet in the room except for the whispers of younger people translating to their parents. Kev shared a few funny stories and had all of us laughing. I was so proud of him for bringing the relief of joy to the service.

Afterward, in the parking lot, the people who spoke to Keven complimented or thanked him for his words. Gilberto's mother, wife and kids surrounded him. I remember his oldest son shaking Keven's hand and his daughter and younger son holding on to Keven's legs as if they didn't want him to leave, a touching scene I will never forget. Afterward, the three of us drove home in silence.

Another young man, Michael, moved in with Therese and me after Anthony passed away, and we loved having him here. Like so many, he was doing great in his sobriety—until he wasn't. We had to ask Michael to move out. He'd still drop by to visit and would often play his guitar for us, singing songs from our era that his dad had taught him—Cat Stevens, The Beatles, Jim Croce, Johnny Cash. At the time, Keven was doing a stint in prison, so it was the next best thing to having him home. A few years later, Michael's roommate found him dead in his bedroom. He'd been there for a few days.

Then there was John. He and Keven met at a rehab called Unidos ("united" in Spanish). John was using heroin to cope with PTSD after serving in Iraq but had finally got some sober time. Keven and I were driving him up to the Veteran's Hospital one afternoon, and he opened up to me about his life after the military.

This young man had served his country, risked his life in battle and came back broken by the things he'd seen and done. He was discharged for psychiatric conditions and came home to nothing. He started using heroin to escape his thoughts and feelings and then eventually made his way to recovery.

"When I was discharged, my dad wanted nothing to do with me—and he's the only family I have. The doctors put me on Haldol, so I felt like I was living in a fog. I couldn't get a job because I wasn't capable of thinking straight, so with no family and no way to support myself, I ended up on the streets. Everybody out there is using heroin. They offered it to me for free, so I started getting high. But after a few weeks, it wasn't free anymore, so I had to steal to support the habit." He sounded so ashamed. "I got busted and was dope sick in jail. I thought I was going to die because they wouldn't do anything to help me get through it. Then I was offered a county-paid bed at Unidos, and that's where I met your son." He smiled as he mentioned Keven.

"You've got a good one here, Miss Legere," John said as he slapped Keven on the back of the head. I was proud of the person Keven was, the real person. I couldn't be proud of Keven's actions while using drugs, but I never stopped being proud of my son's true self.

I looked into John's eyes and sincerely thanked him for his service to our country. He responded: "No one has ever said that to me before. Thank you. It means a lot."

How could that be true? This young man was fine before he went to Iraq, and now his life was ruined because of his service. After John experienced the normal human responses to trauma, the Marines discharged him for having mental health issues. John had nothing. No one was helping him. I had to fight the urge to invite him to live with us. I had done that several times with others and learned the hard way it wasn't always the smart thing to do.

A year later, Keven said to me, "Hey, Mom, guess who died now? John." I looked up at him and searched Keven's face. He had lost so many friends by this time, and it just didn't surprise him anymore. But it still hurt. I cried hard that night, wondering if there would even be a service for him. There wasn't.

Then there was sweet, beautiful Kelly. She was another person who was full of energy and smiled all the time. Kelly and Keven were often mistaken for brother and sister. Not only did they look alike—both tall and slender with dark hair and glasses —but they acted like siblings too. She fit right in with our family and visited often. We all loved her, and our pets adored her. She was an animal person and worked as a dog groomer.

Kelly did so well when she tried. She had long periods of sobriety—one time for more than a year. We enjoyed going shopping together or to lunch. But, as often is the case, something in Kelly's life triggered depression, and she started using again to numb the pain.

I ran into Kelly one afternoon in the parking lot of a grocery store. She smiled as she approached, and I could see even from a distance the glossy eyes, dirty hair and wrinkled clothing. As she hugged me, she said, "I'm the happiest I've ever been! I found my new way of life, and I love it."

"I got a tent!" Kelly was eager to explain, "I live under the bridge. I get high whenever I want to. I always get drugs or money when I need it; no one can tell me what to do or not do!" Her face was smiling, but her light was gone.

Before I could find the words to respond, Kelly turned and walked away, saying, "Tell Kev and the fam I said hi!" I watched her disappear down the street toward the bridge.

Keven and Kelly, Clean and Sober Together

Six years later, I found out from her mother that she had died by suicide in jail on the East Coast. I couldn't imagine this feisty and stubborn young woman giving up on anything. I couldn't accept that she hung herself in her cell over a theft charge. I never told her mom this, but when I got in touch with Kelly's boyfriend, the first words out of his mouth were, "They killed her!" He explained what he believed really happened: she was murdered by a guard. We will never know for sure, and the truth wouldn't bring her back.

There are also happy endings in the lives of Anthony and Keven's friends. There's Joshua, who got out of prison, found a job and has developed a loving, healthy relationship with his young daughter. I see them on Facebook and think everyone should have such a loving dad.

Ray realized he'd never get it together if he stayed in this area. So he moved to Oregon with his girlfriend, had a baby and started a successful business. He's doing great in all areas of his life.

Jamie, an ex-girlfriend of Kev's, had three young children taken away from her because of her Substance Use Disorder. But after working a program for women, Jamie found lasting sobriety and got custody of her kids back, met a great guy and got married.

Matt M., who was the only true friend Keven met while in jail, got a job straight out of prison and has been living a healthy lifestyle ever since. He was there for me after Keven passed, checking in on me daily and visiting when he could. He's faced several tragedies in the last few years but hasn't turned back to drugs to cope. He stays very busy—I've heard a lot of people say that's the key to staying sober.

When Anthony died, he left behind a group of young women: Cheryl, Gabrielle, Presley, Cheyanne and Kelli.

They helped me grieve his passing and my life is richer for having them in it.

Cheryl has this to say about her recovery:

"I have been sober for ten years from heroin and meth. I still struggle on and off, but I've been able to push through and continue the fight. I'm regimented in taking my meds and attend weekly or twice-weekly therapy. Finding doctors who truly understand and accept what and who I am has been vital. I did eight years of AA, then relapsed but pulled myself up with the fear of the past and everyone who has died."

Cheryl has lost some of the most important people in her life and has learned to move forward through the pain, as all of us do. What choice do we have?

CHAPTER 11
SOCIAL STIGMA OF SUBSTANCE ABUSE AND MENTAL ILLNESS

> *This stigma associated with drug use—the belief that bad kids use, good kids don't, and those with full-blown addiction are weak, dissolute and pathetic—has contributed to the escalation of use and hampered treatment more than any other single factor.*
>
> ~David Sheff

Woven together, the lives of friends that Keven made over the years in and out of recovery make a tapestry of pain, loss, hope, love, despair, trauma and recovery. Some are still here; many are gone. I cherish each of their lives as a precious gift, and I hope they realize how much I appreciate their trust. They have helped me to understand what it is like for someone dependent on heroin. I wouldn't be here, still standing and breathing after such unspeakable loss, if it weren't for them and our shared trust.

I am always heartbroken when I discover how cruel people can be to substance users, calling them losers or junkies. These are human beings and should not be dismissed as "just another addict." They are so much more. They are good people who make bad choices. Their choices are often the result of trauma and despair that we can't fathom. Their drug use may have altered their outward behavior but didn't change their inner selves. No one grows up with the goal of struggling with substance use. We all start out the same—with hopes, dreams, plans and the need to be loved.

In addition to their constant regrets for relapse, all the kids I got to know whose lives touched mine and Keven's felt constant guilt and dread for disappointing their families, especially their parents. They lied, stole, flunked out of school, couldn't keep a job and felt like failures over and over again. All of these things ate away at their core. Many of these young people were the oldest children in their families and could no longer be role models for their siblings. They all lost friends to overdose, but it didn't slow down their drug use. The nature of Substance Use Disorder is such that death becomes just one more risk they are willing to take. Each of them comes from different circumstances, but their experiences are much the same.

Stigma is a large part of the problem. Society views people suffering from Substance Use Disorder horribly, and these people who need our care are treated poorly. Social stigma only makes the way people feel about themselves and their problems worse, eating away at their dignity and hope. It causes feelings of isolation and creates a reluctance to ask for or accept help or seek treatment. I saw with my own eyes how doctors and medical professionals treated Anthony and Keven. Because of the time taken away from other patients and the growing number of overdose cases, an ER doctor at Mission Hospital once said to Keven, Therese and me, "I don't know why I should be bothered to help your son. He's an addict; he's going to end up dead anyway. He's taking my time away from helping people who really need it." We understood why he said it, but it still hurt to hear.

Law enforcement was the same way. It seems like I've met every police officer in Mission Viejo, and 50 percent of them made it clear that substance users were an unsavory blight on society and that they deserved the worst kind of treatment.

Having been on the frontlines in the battle to save my son's life over and over again, I found that many judges and attorneys actually have empathy for people in Keven's position. But one of Keven's public defenders said to us, "Your son is going to keep on using, and I can tell you right now he's a lost case." Imagine being told at every turn that you are hopeless, worthless and deserve to die. Imagine the impact that would have on a *healthy* person, let alone one who is fighting for his life and losing.

As published in his article "Turning Grief into Active Compassion" in *Psychology Today* (August 5, 2020), here is what David Sheff, author of the bestselling book *Beautiful Boy*, has to say about stigma:

I frequently hear from parents whose kids are currently addicted or have died of overdose. Some of them are consumed by pain and bitterness; they live in a state of hell. I don't judge them. I understand. I'd be there right with them. But then there are people whose grief evolves into a useful kind of anger. Many of those who die of addiction do so because they've been failed by what passes for a mental-health care system in America.

They also die because of the stigma of addiction—they keep their problem hidden because of shame—until there are devastating consequences. And they often don't get any treatment whatsoever. "Oh, he's just a junkie." An ER nurse told me that she hears doctors say it all the time. Many are deprived of addiction medications that could save their lives. Many parents or other loved ones recognize the broken system and determine to do whatever they can to prevent other parents from having to endure the suffering they've endured. They're passionately committed to improving the treatment system, educating about addiction, and lobbying legislators for support for those suffering mental illness. The ability to create change, even if it comes a small shift at a time, is empowering. No parent will ever stop grieving the loss of a child, but these men and women find new purpose.

One day, I came home from a trip to the grocery store with Keven. He'd been using for days and was starting to detox. It was obvious by the way he walked, his crumpled clothes and his demeanor that there was something "off" about him. For most mothers and sons, the grocery store is an eventless outing. But for me, being in the public eye at times like this, I felt judged and looked down upon. I put down a few words when I arrived home:

He's my son; I love him.
I see the stares and hear the whispers behind his back.
I'm aware of the opinions of people that know us.
I can imagine the conversations about enabling, tough love and the list of ways my parenting is faulty.
Yes, he's a grown man on the outside.
Yes, he looks different: the way he walks, the glaze in his half-closed eyes, unkempt appearance, stained fingers.
Yes, he sounds different; he mumbles at times.
He's not "slow," and he's not "a slob." He has access to clean clothes and a shower.
He's intelligent, kind, thoughtful and loving.
His pain is deep, his anxiety debilitating.
He's not a criminal, but he is a felon.
He's not allowed at family events.
He has few friends and no social life.
His guilt at what he's put me through overwhelms him at times.
He's aware of how judged he is by society, by neighbors, by most people who know us.
He still holds open doors, is polite and would give you his last dollar.
He loves his family and his pets. He has a tender heart.
He does everything he's capable of to make himself less of a "burden" to me.
I try not to relive the moments of terror when I almost lost him.
I stay positive and encouraging and loving on the outside because if he knew the depth of my suffering, he would never get over it.

I don't pray for him anymore because my prayers have gone unanswered year after year.

I still ask others to pray on the slim chance it may help.

He prays; he has a strong Christian faith.

I lost mine years ago.

He is my son. I love him with all my heart. I'm proud of him, even though no one else may understand why.

I've accepted the way things are but hope they don't stay this way much longer.

I know I may lose him, but he will never lose me. As long as I'm breathing, I'll be here for him.

I don't make sacrifices for him—I willingly do what I need to do to ease his suffering and encourage him.

I get mad, tired, scared, frustrated and stressed out, but I will never lose hope.

He's my son: the little boy who crawled in my lap to snuggle, who brought me joy I didn't know existed.

He also brought me a level of pain I never knew existed. I hurt for him, not because of him.

I politely smile as I listen to your "issues" with your children and your life and secretly think you have no idea how lucky you are.

Yes, I saw that look you gave us today at the store; your face said it all. He didn't notice—this time.

He is my son.

I love him.

I accept him.

I understand him.

If you've never walked in my shoes, shame on you for thinking your children are better than mine.

If you are thankful, you're not in my shoes—good, you should be.

If you are disgusted by the shoes he and I wear, I don't care. I don't waste my time caring what you think, but I do see it. I feel it. I am aware of it.

~Written on 8/18/19 (Keven passed on 8/11/20)

It's my hope that someday people who are lost in substance use—whether they use alcohol, opiates or any other substance—are treated with the same respect that people with diabetes, cancer or other diseases are offered. We all start out the same: innocent with unlimited potential. Life happens between birth and death, and each of us is given different circumstances to be born into and to face in our lives. Some of us can drink alcohol casually and stop when we want; some of us can't. Some try drugs and carry on with life. Others try drugs and discover they can mask whatever pain they are trying to avoid, then find they are tossed into the pit of self-destruction.

His Broken Heart

CHAPTER 12
A DAY IN THE LIFE OF A HEROIN USER

    For many people who take this substance, heroin is more about avoiding or numbing pain than feeling good. Compared to other drugs such as alcohol, marijuana, cocaine and meth, heroin is taken less for recreational and social reasons and more for self-medication.

    ~Elizabeth Hartney, BSc, MSc, MA, Ph.D., *The Feeling of Getting High on Heroin*

Here is what Keven, Anthony and their friends taught me about what life with Substance Use Disorder was like for them.

After using heroin/opiates for a while, you build up a tolerance to it. You need more each time to generate the same high you had in the beginning. Eventually, you aren't even getting very high, but you must keep using to "stay well" and avoid the horrible effects of withdrawal symptoms, also known as being "dope sick."

You want your family and old friends back. You want to be invited to Christmas dinner, family events or to hang out. Your new "friends" are other users; no one else wants to be around you. You've committed crimes and done things that cause shame and humiliation. It's likely you have at least one felony and have done jail time, or worse yet, prison time.

Some people treat you as if you're a low-life who is getting what they deserve. Most people have given up on you, and it hurts.

You're aware that you've messed up your life and promise yourself that you will no longer be controlled by heroin. Heroin is your enemy disguised as your best friend—your lover. You hate what it's done to your life but love how it makes you feel and don't want to live without it.

Every night when you go to bed, you vow that tomorrow will be the day you stop using. When you wake up in the morning, you feel the early signs of dope sickness. You may have a runny nose, restless legs, sensitivity to touch or sore muscles. These are mild annoyances compared to what you know is coming if you don't put some opiates back in your system. If you don't use, the hell of full-blown dope sickness is inevitable.

Each new day it's a race against the clock. In a matter of hours, your symptoms will worsen. You'll feel nauseous and may vomit or have diarrhea, and the body aches will be more intense. A lot of people say they felt so sick they wished they were dead.

You have only one focus: getting more drugs. Once you get your hands on some and shoot up or smoke it, you'll feel better instantly. All will be well with your world, and you can continue with your day.

You've tried to detox countless times before but have rarely been able to get through it on your own. For a successful detox, you need medication to lessen your symptoms. If you don't have insurance or money to pay to go to a medical detox, you suffer through it.

Often you decide to just get enough heroin for today, so you can feel well. You tell yourself that you can start to detox tomorrow. So now you must "go on a mission" to obtain more drugs, which could take a few hours or all day. The longer it takes, the worse you feel, so time is of the essence.

The most difficult part of this process is getting the money to buy the dope. There aren't many legal or moral ways to get your hands on cash immediately. (In today's world, with apps like Venmo, it's not always necessary to have cash in hand. It's safer for the buyer and the dealer to not have a lot of cash on them in case they get pulled over.) If you get pulled over and they find a gram or less of heroin, you get charged with possession of a controlled substance. If they also find a scale or wad of cash, they can bust you for sales—a felony that can get you years in prison.

Either way—cash or an app—you still have to find the money. Stealing is the most popular method. You can steal from family, friends, retail stores, unlocked cars and other users. You can steal jewelry or other items to pawn—hot items that are trending to barter with or credit cards to buy merchandise to sell. (One of Keven's many methods was to steal my Shell gas card and offer to fill people's gas tanks for half the normal cost if they paid him cash. He collected a lot of money that way, and I got footed with the bill. I cut the card in half when I figured it out.)

After obtaining the money for the day's purchase, it's time to find the drugs. Most substance users have at least one consistent dealer or "connect" and several back-ups in case that dealer is in jail, out of product or simply not answering their phone that day. On days where your connections come up empty, you can turn to Craigslist. (It is surprisingly simple to find both heroin and meth on Craigslist. The code for heroin is "black tar." Simply entering this into the search bar reveals ads for roofing companies specializing in "black tar roofs"—a giveaway for a dealer's ad. If you're looking for meth, enter the name Chris, Tina or Crystal—up pop the personal ads for meth.)

Now that you have the money and made the deal, it's time to pick up. For those without transportation, this can be tricky. Keven could usually get his hands on a vehicle, but Anthony relied on other people or the bus to get him to Santa Ana or wherever the transaction would take place. If you're lucky, you have a dealer who will meet you halfway—in a parking lot or equally anonymous place. If not, you need to drive to their chosen location, which could change a time or two before you finally meet up. Dealers get paranoid and want to avoid being conspicuous, but they sometimes get another sale and want to meet both customers at the same place.

If you can't find anyone to buy from, you can always get yourself to Santa Ana and drive down one of the many "drug streets." Dealers live on these streets and use kids (their own or from the neighborhood) to run the drugs to the buyers. All you have to do is drive slowly down one of the streets and wait for one of these kids to ride up to you on his bike and ask what you want. You tell him the type of drug and the amount, and they tell you the price. You hand the kid the cash and drive around the block. By the time you circle back, the kid is waiting with your drugs, and the deal is complete.

Finally, the long-awaited ritual of using. This is a sacred experience for substance users. Gathering the supplies, prepping the needle or foil, then injecting or inhaling, followed by the rush of intense pleasure. The high is euphoria. You're free from worry, pain and anxiety. You experience a flood of warmth followed by deep relaxation and detachment from every bad feeling you've ever had. That is, until you need more.

This ritual only loses its appeal when you run out of veins to inject when they collapse from overuse (known as being "shot out"). This means you have to find a muscle to inject—your hips, buttocks, arms or legs. There is grave danger of infection when using this method because bacteria can get caught up in the muscles, working their way into the bloodstream and causing sepsis, a life-threatening infection. When an abscess forms, it must be drained, followed by a round of antibiotics to clear up the infection. Doctor visits and hospital stays only slow down your usage, but if left untreated, you could be faced with the possibility of multiple surgeries at best and losing a limb at worst. If you do need surgery, pain medication is useless. Your tolerance to opiates is so high that a normal dose does nothing.

Other complications include collapsed veins, which means you're unable to draw blood or insert an IV for a medical procedure. In order to find a vein, an ultrasound is needed, but hospital staff aren't always willing, so they'll poke and poke relentlessly, following their normal protocols.

At the end of each day, for those who don't have a permanent home, you need to find a place to rest for the night. This could mean crashing at a friend's place, a motel room with other users or sleeping on the streets somewhere. Hopefully, you will wake up in the morning.

CHAPTER 13

THINGS I NEVER THOUGHT I'D DO

Do what you feel in your heart to be right, for you'll be criticized anyway.

~Eleanor Roosevelt, In Her Words: On Women, Politics, Leadership, and Lessons from Life

The desperation of someone dependent on dangerous substances is torture to witness. Because of my role as mom to Keven and his friends, I found myself in compromising and morally reprehensible situations on many occasions. Did I want to participate in my son's or his friends' illegal drug purchasing? Absolutely not. But I had to choose between the terror of wondering if they were alive or witnessing first-hand how they hustled for their lives.

I have been on drug rides both knowingly and unwittingly. I have been inside "drug houses," a voyeur into the dismal existence of young people living to get high. I have received confessions from young people about the ways they got money to make their buys. Listening to the retelling of these stories helped me understand their desperation while filling me with a frantic concern for their well being

Aside from stealing from loved ones to get money, substance users find dangerous and demoralizing ways to support their habit. Some sell their bodies for money—both men and women, but mostly women. I learned about a scam that Keven and a friend ran on Craigslist, placing ads to find men who wanted to have sex with a younger guy and were willing to pay. One of them would get a hotel room where he'd wait for his "date." The other would wait outside the room with his own room key. When the first guy called out, the other would enter the room and take the mark's money. For insurance against the victim contacting the police, they took photos of the man and his driver's license, intimidating him into silence. This worked every time. It was hard for me to believe this; I felt sick to my stomach hearing it. This was something you'd see on TV, not something my son would do, right?

Keven went to jewelry and watch stores that sold high-end watches. He would dress in his suit and a fine fedora paired with an expensive watch and casually peruse the store. When salesmen discovered how articulate and knowledgeable Keven was, they always took him seriously as a potential buyer. At the time, he could apply for credit and pass the background check, lying about having a steady job. He could typically walk out with a $5-10,000 watch—he had something to sell for cash, and the salesperson had a nice commission. Eventually, the unpaid bills piled up, and the creditors were on to him. It disheartened me that Keven's good morals had been robbed by drugs.

Once when Keven was in jail, I found myself walking willingly into a "drug house." Anthony had borrowed Keven's electric bike, left it there, and I wanted it back so Keven could use it when he got out. I knew of the main guy who lived there named "Pinky." I should have been terrified, but instead, I was depressed. What I saw sat like a rock in my stomach because I knew this was just one example of what was happening all across our country.

"Hey, I'm looking for Pinky," I told the bald guy smoking by the entrance. His skinny, ghost-like frame was shirtless, and he was covered in tattoos, not unlike Anthony and Keven.

"Who are you?" he asked.

"Anthony's mom," I answered.

He nodded and led me into the house. I waited in the front room while he found Pinky. In the dark, I could make out the shapes of beat-up couches and chairs pulled from garbage piles around the city. People were draped like forgotten jackets, two or three deep in various stages of getting high or coming down. A man was injecting a pregnant girl in her neck. I had met this girl once. She knew she was pregnant and that the baby would be taken from her; she didn't care if her baby was born addicted to opiates. My heart was full of despair.

Pinky slunk out of the back, acting the cordial host, shaking my hand and offering me something to drink. He was bald, overweight and looked mean. "I've heard so much about you," he said, "Anthony speaks very highly of you."

Pinky was reluctant to hand over the bike. "You know this is collateral, right? Anthony owes me money."

"Well, that bike doesn't belong to Anthony. I lent it to him. I need it back, so please give it to me. I don't want any problems." It sounded like a threat, and I knew I couldn't back it up or take it back.

He considered all this and miraculously gave me the bike.

"Anthony's one of the good ones—that's the only reason I'm doing this. I owe him one, but he still owes me money." I thanked Pinky and quickly left.

I also helped Keven pick up drugs in a strip-mall parking lot on more than one occasion. There were the times I knew what I was doing: helping Keven score "one last time" as a condition for him willingly entering rehab. But there were also times I unknowingly accompanied Keven on deals. One time we were across the street from his parole office following a drug test. After testing negative, Kev asked if he could get a burger, so we stopped at McDonald's. He insisted on eating it in the car, and as I waited for him to finish eating, I noticed he was texting some-one. A lot. He eventually admitted that his dealer had several clients in this parking lot and was hitting car after car, finishing deals. Most likely, all of them had been visiting their parole officer prior to buying. It was a different type of drive-up service, convenient for everyone.

There was a point in time I would have been horrified with the thought of a parent providing drugs to their addicted child. But that time had come and gone. If Keven would not go to rehab without getting high, I saw it as an opportunity for him to get help, a last resort, my only hope. Only a few people in my life knew this; I feared being judged or rejected by other parents. Now it's an example of how desperate a parent can become to get their child help—how willingly they will do the unthinkable if they believe it will lead to sobriety.

I rarely shared this part of my story with anyone. I knew that to an outsider, it sounded like the ultimate act of enabling. On the few occasions I did mention it, it brought me some comfort to know I wasn't alone. There were other parents out there doing the same thing. We would do anything to help our children get one step closer to getting help and going to rehab.

Would I do it again? Do I think it helped or harmed Keven? The answer to both is, "I don't know." It helped him get into rehab. I wasn't increasing the harm because he would have found a way to find drugs on his own if I hadn't been there. When you're in a moment of desperation, you make in-the-moment decisions that could have any number of outcomes.

I feel ashamed of my actions, but at the same time, I had only my instincts to act upon in the moment. The bottom line for me was my motivation: every decision I made was purely for Keven's greater good. But having good intentions doesn't necessarily mean it was the right thing to do. I would not recommend my choices or actions to other parents. But in my mind at the time, it was better to arrive at rehab high than to not arrive at rehab at all.

CHAPTER 14
LOSING ME, FINDING HELP

> *It's very important that we re-learn the art of resting and relaxing. Not only does it help prevent the onset of many illnesses that develop through chronic tension and worrying; it allows us to clear our minds, focus and find creative solutions to problems.*
>
> ~Thich Nhat Hanh

After the first few years of knowingly living with a substance user who was in and out of court, jail, prison, rehab and sober living, I came to a place where —as Bruce Springsteen says in his song, "Philadelphia"—I was unrecognizable to myself. Who was this woman filled with fear, confusion, resentment and anger? How had I put on 50 pounds? Why did my muscles ache, and when did I become constantly exhausted? Why did I develop hives? Where was the old me hiding?

Worry about Keven and Anthony and my own guilt and self-doubt consumed me day and night. I was always trying to figure out how to help Keven or wondering where he was and whether he'd come home alive. I knew by now how recovery worked: he had to want the help. But maybe I could help him want it? I constantly ruminated on what I should have done or could do differently next time to prevent his substance use. My self-punishment only served to deepen my depression.

When morning finally broke after each sleepless night, the physical, mental and emotional exhaustion hit like a tsunami before my feet even touched the floor. I'd stare at the ceiling, my dog Sugar snoring blissfully next to me, and listen to the squawking crows for as long as I could before getting up for work. Was Keven home? Was he awake? Was he alive?

My reputation for being an easy-going, fun person was long gone. When a co-worker or friend asked, "How's it going?" I always gave them an update on Keven. My life and his inter-twined like a pair of shoelaces; sometimes tight, sometimes undone, but always crossed and knotted in confusion.

Even with my closest work friends, I never divulged half of what went on with Kev. The majority of my co-workers were conservative Christians, and they weren't familiar with the complicated world of substance use. By now, I had been working for this organization for 17 years—they had watched my boy grow up. It shocked them to see him go from Legos to syringes. To me, he was still and always would be my beautiful child, but very few people saw him that way now. And I was certain that in their minds, I was to blame for Keven's problems.

When I first started working at my job in 1991, one woman complained to HR that they had hired a single mom with a newborn. This was sinful in her eyes, so imagine what she thought of me now! While I did my best not to care what my co-workers thought of me, I did care that they didn't understand my son.

I could have hidden my problems and kept our struggles secret, but I was never ashamed of Keven. It sounds odd to say I was proud of him when he was causing so much stress and drama in my life. My love for Keven was unconditional, and I was proud of who I knew he *really* was. If others could only see past the drugs, they could see his worth, too. When I did open up about our ups and downs, it was because I wanted these well-meaning people to know about the opioid epidemic happening across our country. My situation wasn't an isolated incident. At the time, very little was being reported in the media, and people didn't know.

"I'm glad I raised my kids right; they're all in college now," was a common refrain. I wanted desperately to explain that "not my kid" are the three most dangerous words a parent could utter, but I knew my warnings wouldn't get through. People can't hear you when they refuse to listen.

Growing up in a loving, religious family doesn't guarantee anything. Nearly every substance user I've ever met came from an upper-middle-class home in a nice neighborhood where they were cared for with love, attention and discipline. They had all been warned repeatedly about drug use.

My co-workers weren't educated on the topic; they didn't know any better. No parent imagines their child on life support with a ventilator breathing for them after they were left for dead in an alley. When your child is seven years old and you're wrapping presents from Santa, you don't think about the possibility of them in a hospital with tubes inserted. You don't suddenly envision your beloved child's body connected to a pump to drain an infection stemming from an untreated abscess from needle use following three surgeries in seven days. You can't even believe it's real when you are living it! But believing that substance use only happens to *other people's children* is naïve and dangerous. If every parent is aware of the dangers of drug use, then my deepest hope in sharing our experiences is that it might open eyes, leading others to be compassionate.

Eventually, I lost my job. My boss and friend Virginia sat on the edge of my desk and looked at me. We knew each other well, so her expression did the talking for her.

"I'm fired?" I asked, trying not to get emotional.

"No, sweetie, it's a lay-off. You're not the only one." I knew she was being kind, and this was confirmed years later when she confessed that my performance was indeed a factor. Heat rose to my face. I was embarrassed that it had come to this. I was at one time an excellent employee, but now I had become a liability. I lacked focus and made too many mistakes.

I needed to get my life back on track and not let Keven be the center of my world. Even though I felt like I was losing everything in my life, including my son, I had to find myself.

CHAPTER 15

THE TROUBLE WITH TOUGH LOVE

> *We've been approaching addiction improperly for a long time, and "tough love" is a huge part of our mistake, in my opinion. Although boundaries are important, and sometimes we have to be tough with ourselves to keep the boundaries in place, traditional tough love is still shaming and reflects a paradigm of addiction that doesn't honor the love and care that those with addiction need.*
>
> ~Eric Nada, MA, LMFT

"Barbara, I don't think it's a good idea that you let Keven have a car."

"Hey hon, is it a good idea to let Keven live with you?"

"You seriously should let him figure this out on his own."

"He'll never get better unless he hits rock bottom; kick him out."

Everyone has an opinion. I heard that last one the most. People don't really understand that with substance users, there is no "rock bottom" except for death. Whatever their bottom is today, it can always sink lower—until they're gone. I'd rather my son die at home, knowing that I did everything I could to save him than for him to die on the street anonymously.

What well-meaning people need to understand about parenting substance users is that we question every decision we make. Unable to hear another friend's or relative's inexperienced advice, I usually got quiet and simply responded, "Thanks for your concern," before walking away.

In my desperation and isolation, I started writing a blog called *The Needle and the Damage Done*. Through this online journaling, I was able to connect with other parents around the country who were navigating and surviving the torture of parenting substance users. We formed a tight-knit community that made us feel less alone. Many of us are still close today.

"I can't do this anymore! I need to make a drastic change before this stress takes me out," I vented to another parent who had started writing a blog. We were an allied front in the war against our children and their substance use.

Annette, Tori, Joy, Lori, Ron, Lou, Renee, Denise, Monica, Sheri, Adrienne, Lisa, Dawn and Helga—the list goes on. These loving parents confirmed for me that what Keven and I were going through wasn't unique and that, indeed, it was happening all over our country. We didn't always agree with each other, but we always listened with respect and an open mind.

We commiserated and shared ideas, prayed and worried. We were there for each other through all the challenges. We welcomed anyone into this group—a club that no one wanted to be a part of.

Although I was drowning in a murky sea, grasping for a life preserver, I had avoided Al-Anon all this time. Even though a lot of parents in the blogging community recommended attending meetings, I was hesitant because I don't like the "one size fits all" approach. Every situation is unique, I reasoned, and unless you've been in my *exact* pair of shoes and understand Keven's unique problems, how could you know what was best for him or me?

Eventually, I relented. In 2011, Keven was 21 and had been in and out of more rehabs and jails than I could count. I could use all the emotional support I could get. It was just the lifeline I needed at the time—I learned that the whole point of Al-Anon is to practice using tools to help yourself so that you are not absorbed by the life of your loved one. In Al-Anon, I learned how to put myself first and not let substance users control my life. But it wasn't going to be easy.

Saturday mornings at 8 am, I attended an Al-Anon group just for parents. Donna had been going since her daughter, Anthony's mom, had started using. Now she went because of Anthony and Timmy .

As an introvert with social anxiety, walking into that first meeting was an act of sheer will. I forced myself out of the house, into the car and through the church doors. In a back room, I found a big circle of folding chairs, and on the floor in the center of the circle were cards with phrases like, "Let go, Let God," "One Day at a Time" and "Keep Coming Back." There were two long tables in the back with books, brochures, coffee and bagels.

Strangers were milling about, chatting over paper coffee cups and disposable plates. Conversations and laughter filled the room, and everyone seemed to know each other. My heart was pounding as I scouted out the chair farthest from the others, where I felt like I could hide.

I didn't want anyone to know that I was new (but came to find out that order number one when the meeting opens is for newcomers to raise their hands). I scanned the room, trying not to break out in a sweat. The woman sitting next to me was deep in conversation with her neighbor. I left my purse on the chair and stood in line for a cup of coffee so that by the time I got back to my seat, the meeting would start, and I wouldn't be obligated to interact with anyone.

Standing in the coffee line, I saw a few people who looked familiar: a very healthy-looking couple I would eventually meet when I started going to yoga classes, a short guy around my age who may have been someone I went to high school with. Most of us were around the same age. The man in front of me turned and smiled, introducing himself as Dave. He pointed to the book table and told me to be sure to check out the free brochures.

The meeting started. The leader emphasized the importance of attending six meetings in order to determine whether you like it or not. That made sense to me. But the most powerful thing I heard at that first meeting was that all parents of substance users need to remember the "Three Cs of Al-Anon": You didn't Cause it, you can't Control it and you can't Cure it.

Every person in that room had a different story, yet we were all the same. It was the first time I had been around people, in person, who understood what I was going through. There's great comfort in finding your people. That's why I kept attending weekly meetings, eventually got a sponsor and worked the 12 steps. I finally knew I was not alone. I shared my story, made friends and began healing.

A common disagreement in our meetings eventually created an ugly division. The issue was the concept of "tough love." One camp believed you had to cut off your kid 100 percent—no contact, no calls, no texts and no help with living expenses. The rest of us thought that was too harsh.

Defining "tough love" is nearly impossible because everyone has a different opinion about it. My understanding of the concept is the act of completely cutting off your loved one: no contact, no financial or emotional support until they have proven their lasting sobriety and are working toward repairing their mistakes. The idea of enabling also has many definitions, but to me, it means doing things for the substance user that they should or could be doing for themselves. But even this is too broad a definition for some; to avoid enabling, does it mean not buying cigarettes for someone even if they can't get a job to pay for their own? Groceries? What about supporting your grandchildren—does that fall under the category of enabling the substance users? The lines are blurry to begin with, and in my experience, they changed with time.

John was a big guy with thick gray hair and a permanent scowl. He was very vocal about his opinions and repeated, "Anyone who allows their addicted adult child to live with them is enabling them. They will never get better till you kick them out of your house and let them hit bottom." This didn't sit well with the half of us who generally rejected broad statements like this. There are too many unique circumstances. John made me angry because opinions aren't facts.

Then there was the couple that announced with pride, "We kicked our son out three years ago and haven't talked to him since." I couldn't understand how this was a good thing! I loved my son more than anything, and not talking to Keven for three years was unthinkable! Sure, I wouldn't have to live with his daily chaos, and it would save me a ton of money if I wasn't financially supporting him, but those were sacrifices I willingly made to keep my son in my life and alive.

On the other end of the spectrum, there were parents whose adult children had been living with them for years and were on a constant cycle of using, recovery and relapse. This group of parents was labeled "enablers." I was part of that group.

I make no apologies for rejecting the idea of tough love. Keven and I were extremely close because he had no father and no siblings—it was just us. He was proud to call himself a "mama's boy." I continued to attend meetings, hoping to find a more balanced approach to parenting and letting go that would be healthier for both of us. But hearing the phrase, "Kick him out and let him hit rock bottom" over and over made me doubt myself. Was I wrong? Maybe I was doing the opposite of helping Keven.

I also heard the saying, "Don't love your substance users to death." To this day, those words haunt me. I let Keven live with me and helped him every single time he asked. And then he died. I still don't believe that my love for my son caused his death. Drugs caused his death. Without my love, would he have lived as long? This is just another question for which there is no answer, even today.

Even having lost my child, I stand by my decision not to abandon him through his struggle with drugs. I still don't believe this is the solution to SUD, alcoholism or mental health issues. Users are vulnerable and need to feel loved, supported and understood. I believe that I would have lost Keven much sooner if I'd turned my back on him. While the tough love approach works for some, there is truly no one-size-fits-all approach to recovery and how to love someone through their struggles with substance use.

As a caveat, I know that it's different for some families. If Keven had been violent or if I had other children to consider, I would have needed a different approach to protect myself or others in my home.

Eventually, our Al-Anon meeting was fractured beyond repair, and John and his group split from ours over the tough love issue. They started their own separate meeting, which I believe brought more harmony for all of us.

I have noticed that opinions have been changing in the last few years, or maybe with more awareness, more people are feeling confident about sharing their thoughts and experiences using the tough love approach. Here are some thoughts on the topic from a group I follow on Facebook where some members are substance users in recovery and others are the loved ones of those with SUD. While these are anecdotal experiences, out of 354 comments on this thread alone, the majority agreed that tough love was not the solution:

I'm a recovering addict and if it wasn't for the support and patience my family had for me while I was in active addiction I wouldn't be where I am now! I have 21 months and couldn't have done this without the support I have! The people that stand by us through those tough times and never give up hope are our true HEROES!!!!
~Jessica

Putting an addict in jail doesn't help in any way at all. It all comes down to the addict and how bad they want to recover and have a better life. Then there are some that are so broken they can never be fixed.
~Robin

We did tough love for over 2 years with our daughter and lost her anyway!!!! I even had her put in jail then rehab and she walked out after a week and was gone a week later. The last time I saw her alive I was visiting her in jail!!! Broken hearted forever.
~Nancy's mom, Dawn

I think there's a fine line between loving someone and enabling them... Loving someone through their addiction looks much different than enabling them through their addiction. I think that's where everyone here is getting lost. It's okay to show an addict love. It's not okay to provide them with things they could easily have if they weren't actively using. So, if someone is allowing you to live rent free, steadily giving you money, allowing you to do things around them and providing you with a life that allows you to continue getting high... you will not get better. Why? Because you don't have to! I missed hanging out with my sister, watching my niece and my son grow up daily, just being a part of her and my son's life and actually remembering it all.
~Trish

Yes, it's important to set boundaries but tough love isn't what saved me. I'd be dead now without the unconditional love and attention I received from my parents. I'm going on three years sober and I know if my daughters were ever in my place, I'd fight for their lives how my parents fought for mine.

Rock bottom is a coffin. Period. Dead kids don't have a chance at harm reduction, tapering for moderation, abstinence-based recovery, medication, counseling or any of the other multiple paths to becoming healthier. Seriously. Ask the 93,000+ we lost last year...

I have a recommendation you might try:

*The next time you see your loved ones and they are not in chaos, do
your best to not say one word about substances. Not one word. Try to
listen. Tell them about your day. Ask what they miss about living at
home. Tell them a story about when they were little and loved unconditionally. Remind them of how much you love them. But most of all,
listen. To whatever they say. Doesn't matter what they're saying today,
or even if it's true...you can correct them again tomorrow.*
*Make sure when they leave your presence, you both know how much
each of you are loved. For some of us, that is the only blessing in losing
our loved ones...that they knew they were loved."*
~Stephanie

The most heartbreaking thing for me to read is comments
from parents who tried tough love and lost their child anyway.
They did what they had been told to do by experts and family
alike. Tough love has become common knowledge in and out of
the recovery community and is often believed to be the only
option. These parents who followed cookie-cutter advice in their
approach cannot be blamed. They did what they were told
would help their child. Truthfully, there is no silver bullet solution to Substance Use Disorder; every situation, every person
and every family is different.

It's worth mentioning that I *did* try the tough love approach. I
kicked Keven out of my home many times over the years. I
remember one time we were on our way to rehab when he
announced that he had changed his mind, which naturally led to
a huge argument. I was furious, frightened, let down and
betrayed. So, 40 miles from home, I pulled over on the side of the
road and left him there. I didn't answer his calls for several days.
He eventually made his way home, and we started over—again.

When Keven was on the street, he found other substance
users to stay with. When a group of substance users gets
together, they typically end up in a motel room or somewhere

getting high, committing crimes to pay for their drugs and endangering their health. Let me say clearly: I understand and support the families that had no choice but to remove their child from home, especially with younger kids still living there, but it went against my own maternal instincts. It didn't work for me.

At this point in my life, I had faced the brutal reality that I could lose Kev. I knew he might wind up a statistic, one of the many who didn't make it. The opioid epidemic was finally getting national attention, so it was common knowledge that all over the country, people were dying every day from overdose or drug-related death. I didn't want my child to die alone in a motel room, in an alley or anywhere other than at home. I wanted to be the one to find him rather than getting a middle-of-the-night call from a stranger. I wanted Keven to be surrounded by love up to the last moment of his life. I made a very conscious decision to reject the idea of tough love and to support my son with compassion, boundaries and love.

After two years of attending meetings, I stopped going to Al-Anon. Defending my unpopular views only added to the exhaustion of my daily life, and I was tired of feeling judged. Little did I know then, but my dark journey was still in its infancy. My struggles would continue for many more years. I have no regrets about trying Al-Anon. I picked up some helpful information about caring for myself while caring for Keven. But I didn't feel supported by what felt like a rigid set of beliefs. In a room full of people who only wanted to help each other, I mostly felt like I was traveling alone.

Al-Anon has brought comfort, support and help for countless individuals and families over the years. It truly does work for some. It worked for me in many ways, but eventually, I determined that it didn't provide a solution for my family (though ultimately, nothing could). I hope that the organization and its members continue to evolve as we come to understand more and more about SUD and the various ways people can recover.

CHAPTER 16
FINDING SOLACE

> *The reality is that you will grieve forever. You will not 'get over' the loss of a loved one; you'll learn to live with it. You will heal and you will rebuild yourself around the loss you have suffered. You will be whole again but you will never be the same. Nor should you be the same nor would you want to.*
> ~Elisabeth Kübler-Ross

Shortly after losing Anthony in 2015, I decided to try a new support group I'd heard of that was started by a local woman named Maggie. I knew her from my blog community but had never met her in person. Maggie started the group after losing her son, Mitch, in 2010. After attending many grief support groups for parents, she found that she was treated with less compassion and empathy than others—as if her pain over the loss of Mitch wasn't as valid as a parent's who lost a child to cancer or an accident. She decided that there was a need for a specific group for those who had lost their children to drugs.

Maggie bravely and unselfishly created a space for others who were hurting and grieving from overdose deaths. By founding Solace for Hope, Maggie provided a safe, comforting and healing place for people who have lost a loved one to drugs or love someone that currently suffers with Substance Use Disorder. Maggie has been an inspiration to me for years. I know I speak for hundreds of people when I say she has given us the gift of a community where compassion and understanding flow abundantly. Solace for Hope started out as a small group and has grown to three meeting places in Southern California over the nine years since its founding. It is now a non-profit organization with a private Facebook group that has brought comfort and hope to hundreds.

Meetings are held weekly and last for two hours. The first Solace meeting I attended following Anthony's death felt similar to my first Al-Anon meeting, but this time there was the added fear that because Anthony wasn't my birth son, I wouldn't belong. Would they understand how much I loved him? I understood that the pain was different, but I hoped others in the group would still hold a place for me to mourn.

The room was set up similarly to Al-Anon meetings, with large rectangular tables facing each other. There were about 20 people in that first meeting, and I was approached right away by a woman who welcomed me. Her name was Aimee, and she spoke with a British accent. Her face was both serious and kind. She quickly became one of my heroes when I found out that she spent her Saturdays volunteering for the Orange County Needle Exchange, a group that also handed out NARCAN. Sadly, after a few years, the City of Santa Ana shut it down, claiming that "too many syringes were being left out in public" after being used. They didn't permit the Orange County Needle Exchange to implement the needed changes: providing more consistent safe sharps disposals, community needle sweeps and a hotline to report improperly discharged syringes.

Aimee asked what brought me to the meeting. This opened the flood gates, and I told her, "I lost someone who was like a son to me." She ushered me to a seat, and when the meeting began, I was allowed to share first. As I talked about Anthony, I could feel compassion surrounding me like a warm blanket. Aimee gently touched my arm every now and then, encouraging me with a knowing nod.

Looking through my tear-filled eyes, I saw a few fellow moms were crying along with me. It felt like I had found a new home. One woman, Jeannette, knew Anthony! Her son, Kyle, had given him a tattoo only weeks before he passed. She shared with the group what a great kid he was and how upset her son was about his death. Jeanette would later play a role in Keven's life. It meant so much to me that she validated what a special guy Anthony was. I think all parents appreciate hearing positive things about their kids, but in the case of a substance user, the words were even more meaningful. We all felt that we were living in a society that saw no value in these lives.

Not long after starting Solace, Maggie realized there was also a need for parents who had children still caught up in drug use to find compassion and comfort, so she opened the group to them as well. Now I was attending for both reasons: losing a child dear to me and having a child who was still struggling with Substance Use Disorder.

There is nothing, absolutely nothing, that can substitute for being surrounded by others who understand you. This connection is particularly important when you are a parent who has lost a child to overdose or when you are living with the daily terror of losing one. Although Anthony was not my biological son, these parents accepted me and treated me the same for my loss. My love for Anthony was evident, as was my pain from losing him, but I never for one moment forgot how much deeper their pain was as parents experiencing child loss. I knew I was getting only a taste of the horror of what it would be like if I lost Keven. In many ways, I believe I was drawn to these meetings to develop a network of support for the day that I would eventually lose Keven.

A local drug treatment program sent a group of young men to our meetings, requiring them to attend as part of their recovery. It was important for these substance users to experience how their choices impacted the lives of those who loved them and to hear the parents' perspectives directly. These groups of young men became familiar faces at our Solace meetings. One meeting was never enough. They always came back.

The Solace parents were there to provide love and encouragement, not to judge these troubled young men, and in exchange, these men developed genuine relationships with healthy adults who were not their immediate family, which made it easier for them to have a broader perspective. It was painful for the young men to see the tears, frustration and pain coming from this group of moms and dads, knowing that their own parents were suffering similarly. In our group, these men weren't held responsible for the tears and the pain those tears represented, but they were able to see how their own actions impacted others. I believe it was especially hard for them to witness the agonizing pain of a mother who had just lost a child, knowing that if they were to die, they would cause a similar reaction in their own moms.

The faces would change over time as some young men graduated and new ones entered the program. These guys contributed so much to our group, often helping a mom or dad understand that there was nothing they could have done differently in raising their child. The parents were not to blame for how they handled having a son or daughter abusing heroin, meth or alcohol. They validated our parenting choices and gave us a glimpse into their lives, of what it was like being controlled by a substance. It was truly a win-win arrangement, and we all valued each other's presence and contribution to our shared healing.

These young men always stayed after meetings for hugs and to talk. They became my favorite part of the meetings, and I grew attached to a few of them. Some moved forward in their recovery, and sadly, some are no longer with us.

I will never forget hearing the news about one of the guys that had been extra special in our group. Matt was like a shining star, full of life and committed to sobriety. The cliché about a smile brightening a room fit him perfectly. I was with a group of other moms when I heard he had passed and felt sick to my stomach. There were tears in everyone's eyes. Even for the Matts out there, the risk of relapse and overdose is always hovering over their best intentions.

The Solace Memorial Garden, A Place to Remember Our Loved Ones

CHAPTER 17
ACCEPTANCE

> *Some people believe holding on and hanging in there are signs of great strength. However, there are times when it takes much more strength to know when to let go and then do it.*
>
> ~Ann Landers, *Wake Up and Smell the Coffee!: Advice, Wisdom and Uncommon Good Sense*

One afternoon I encountered a young man outside a fast-food restaurant. His name was Daniel. He held a small cardboard sign that read, "Hungry, anything helps, God bless you." I smiled at him and reached into my purse to give him a couple of bucks. He smiled back in appreciation. My fingers fumbled through my wallet—I had no cash.

"Hey, can I buy you lunch?" I offered.

Our conversation over the meal began with ease as he shared a bit about himself, his battle with drugs and living on the streets. Then he asked about me. As always, I answered by sharing about Keven and what a heartbreaking journey I was on as his mom. "I feel like I am grieving my son even though he's still living." Tears welled in my eyes as I uttered these words.

Daniel listened intently and seemed to care about my distress. His kind voice asked, "You know the Serenity Prayer, right? It's the acceptance part of it you need to focus on. When you're stressed out all the time and worrying about losing your son, you're fighting against something instead of accepting it. How is that helping you or Keven?"

Of course, I already knew this. Or did I?

Daniel smiled with empathy. "You know you can let go and love at the same time, right?"

I sat back and contemplated his words for a moment before the conversation drifted into a new direction. When he finished eating, I thanked him for his insight, and we parted with a hug.

That evening I sat down to process what Daniel had shared. The Serenity Prayer was a mantra of mine: "God grant me the serenity to accept the things I cannot change, courage to change the things I can and wisdom to know the difference." I had accepted that Keven had many debilitating challenges, so what more was there to accept?

Like a waterfall of truth, I was engulfed by all of the things I had not accepted. I had not accepted that I could not fix or save Keven. On the surface, this seems obvious, but deep down inside, most of my angst could be traced to my nonstop quest to *save my son*—not just help him but *save him*. The thought of losing Keven was a constant panic, and although I believed he had to do the work to save himself, my own actions told another story. I wanted sobriety for him far more than he wanted it for himself.

For years I had been offering solutions: rehab, sober living, Medically Assisted Treatment (MAT) and a few unorthodox methods as well. I'd fought Keven's war for him, losing one battle at a time. If I was to accept that I could not save him, it meant that I could stop fighting. I could focus on loving Keven as he was instead of trying to fix him—to save him. Could I give myself permission to wave the white flag?

When and if Keven was ever ready, I believed he would find his way. And while I watched from the sidelines, I could let go of my endless efforts to save him and accept life as it was. Doing so became my steepest mountain to climb—and there had been plenty of them. Choosing to let go of saving my son put me on constant guard against my old way of thinking and forced me to make choices based on my own needs. It wasn't easy. I tried and failed and tried again.

If I hadn't already had the support of parents seeking new ways of healing, I don't think I would have been ready to hear Daniel's advice. And if I hadn't met Daniel that day and offered to buy him lunch, I don't know where I would be today.

The decision to change and to focus on acceptance slowly shifted my life. Rather than feeling the constant pressure to save Keven, I gradually worried less and smiled more. I could take deeper breaths that weren't choked with worry. My attitude became more positive and grateful, and fresh energy filled my being. Yoga and meditation became an enormous help, physically and mentally. I slept better and started to lose the extra weight. I hadn't focused on self-care for many years. With my new focus on acceptance, though Keven's drug use continued (and I still worried), my life was back on track.

CHAPTER 18

THE PROBLEM WITH DRUG TREATMENT PROGRAMS

Putting trauma work at the front and center of drug treatment makes a big difference. Yet we also need to treat people with empathy and respect outside of treatment. Criminalizing drug users focuses action on drug use rather than the underlying cause.

~Paul Delaney

The biggest obstacle to getting a loved one treatment for substance use is the lack of help available to those without the financial means or adequate insurance coverage. In our society, there's an illusion that drug treatment is there waiting for you when you're ready, but this is only true if you have either substantial PPO insurance or can afford thousands of dollars to enroll in a program. A quick web search showed that today, 90 days of treatment can cost $8,000-$111,000, depending on the location and amenities. TV ads and websites announce, "You're not alone, we're here to help, call today," luring suffering families into believing treatment is accessible to anyone who wants it. This messaging is misleading and offers false hope. Help is often *not* available to those who need it most.

In 1956, the American Medical Association defined alcoholism as a disease and expanded the definition to include addiction in 1987. In 2011, they further defined addiction as a "chronic brain disorder" instead of a behavior problem or the result of an individual making "bad choices." However, insurance companies are still allowed to determine what types of medical treatment they will cover, so even if you can afford good insurance, your coverage for Substance Use Disorder recovery may be limited. Most HMO insurance policies don't pay for treatment.

Unless you're wealthy, eligible for a county-funded bed (typically reserved for those on probation or parole) or have PPO insurance, treatment is out of reach. I know many families who have accrued hundreds of thousands of dollars of debt and others who have spent their retirement savings on treatment for their child or themselves. I personally maxed out my credit cards many times over. When you're desperate to help the person you love, you'll consider almost anything at any cost. But not everyone has the luxury of credit cards to max out.

Here in Orange County, California, the city of Costa Mesa is known as "the capital of drug treatment." Per the Orange County Register, "Costa Mesa has more rehabs per square mile than any other place on Earth" (2015).

Keven went to several treatment facilities in Costa Mesa, at least one of which was eventually shut down for fraudulently billing insurance companies for clients who were no longer receiving treatment. Because this area is known as a recovery destination, people travel from all over the country to find help. But not every individual who enrolls in treatment stays in treatment, so it's inevitable that there's a huge population of homeless drug users in Orange County. Substance users who leave or who are kicked out of rehab in Costa Mesa can walk down any of the main streets and find countless others in the same situation to hook up with. Hotel rooms can be found for cheap and soon become known drug hangouts.

Reports of unscrupulous drug treatment programs have increased in recent years. The public is beginning to understand that many of these facilities exist to collect big bucks from insurance companies rather than help the sick and suffering. Corrupt rehabs not only charge insurance companies for treatment they aren't providing, but they are also paying brokers to find clients. When a patient fails a drug test, the facility releases them without informing the insurance company—but then continues to collect payments. This is happening all over the country.

Thankfully, there are exceptions. Above-board facilities can be found that earnestly do their best to help clients get and stay sober. I personally worked for one of those treatment centers for over a year and am pleased to say I saw staff who genuinely care for the young men and women under their care.

Today there's some controversy regarding the way Alcoholics Anonymous (AA) treats people on any kind of Medically Assisted Treatment (MAT). The most common type of MAT is the use of Suboxone, made up of two chemicals, buprenorphine and naloxone, and was created to treat opioid dependence.

This is my layperson's explanation of how it works:

Suboxone is one of the medications commonly used to lessen withdrawal symptoms and help someone get off heroin or any other opioid. Suboxone mimics some of the effects of opiates, lessening the brain's need for the actual opiate drug but it blocks the opiate receptors so if you were to use heroin or another opiate while on Suboxone, you wouldn't get high.

Suboxone was approved by the FDA in 2003. It comes in a sublingual strip but is also available in pills (Subutex) and an injection (Sublocade). When used correctly under a doctor's care, Suboxone lessens the intensity of withdrawal symptoms and helps get the patient on the road to recovery. It's popular because it's effective and has a high success rate.

Alcoholics Anonymous and Narcotics Anonymous are abstinence-based programs. They don't approve of the use of Suboxone (other than for minimizing detox symptoms) because it's technically a narcotic medication, therefore you are not abstinent if you're using it. They have a general rule regarding the use of MAT: if you're using medications to assist in your recovery, you'll be asked not to share at meetings. These groups have determined that using Suboxone, which has an opiate component, is considered trading one drug for another.

The only success Keven ever had staying off heroin was when he took Suboxone. Sometimes he would sneak it into a treatment facility to give himself a better chance at success, but this usually resulted in him getting kicked out when they found it or when it eventually showed up in a urine test. In my experience of watching Keven and other substance users try to recover, penalizing them for using an effective treatment method doesn't make sense. The point of treatment is to stop using drugs that can kill you. If MAT helps save lives, then why exclude it?

Keven enjoyed going to AA meetings because of the fellowship. He preferred AA over NA because the focus on alcohol was less triggering, but the principles were the same. NA meetings typically meant listening to others share about heroin use and getting high. At NA meetings, Keven was also more likely to be approached by someone selling drugs. He stopped attending AA meetings because of their stance on MAT. If Keven wanted to share at a meeting, he'd either have to lie and say he wasn't using Suboxone or simply sit and listen when he was using it. Since sharing and getting out of your head is a crucial part of recovery, Keven eventually stopped going to AA meetings altogether. While it is true that the 12 steps have helped millions of people obtain sobriety over the years, the program doesn't work for everyone.

To get an insider's perspective on MAT, I spoke with Jeannette Spivey and Mike Brown. After over a decade of attending AA meetings, Mike founded Never Use Alone. He is a SMART recovery facilitator, the Michigan State Lead at Recovery Advocacy Project and an Overdose Prevention Specialist at Harm Reduction Michigan. Here is his take on MAT and AA:

I've never understood why people in traditional recovery programs are so against MAT. AA says it's cheating. I've heard 12-step members judging and criticizing people for using Suboxone, even though it's proven to give you better odds at getting and staying sober.

They promote the idea that substance use disorder is a disease, not a moral failing—yet insist that people not use medications to treat their disease. Instead, they require them to pray and take a moral inventory —as if it were a moral failing.

In the meetings, there's always someone repeating the quote, "the drugs weren't the problem. The drugs were just a symptom of the problem." Yet, if the drugs aren't the problem, then what's wrong with using a drug to assist in a person's recovery?

Most people in the program aren't aware that by refusing to let people use medications to aid in a person's recovery, they're going against what Dr. Bill Wilson (one of AA's founders) originally intended. He asked Dr. Vincent Dole, the creator of methadone, to try to create an analog of methadone that would work for people with alcohol use disorder. They don't mention that in the Big Book or other literature.

How is cheating death, any way possible, EVER a bad thing?

I'm honestly not trying to start an argument here. I spent over a decade in and out of "the rooms" and I'm truly wondering if there's something I missed. Since leaving the program, I started seeing things within it that don't make sense. Much of what they do seems to be very contradictory to what they say.

Jeannette is an RN who works at My MAT Clinic, an outpatient treatment facility run by Dr. David Deyhimy. Jeannette is also a friend—she knew both Anthony and Keven and always went above and beyond to help. Here is My MAT Clinic's philosophy:

Drug addiction is not a moral failing, but rather a chronic and treatable disease of the brain. Unfortunately, stigma and misinformation are all too common in addiction treatment and discourage patients from seeking help, understanding their treatment options and receiving proper evidence-based treatment. This type of misinformation and prej-udice has no place in addiction treatment.

Opioid addiction is a chronic disease. It can't be "cured" in one month—or three—any more than diabetes or asthma can. Yet avoiding necessary treatment for chronic illnesses can lead to severe injury and death. Our outpatient treatment is designed for successful extended care, not an unrealistic short-term fix.

Medical research shows outpatient treatment with MAT is clearly superior to abstinence-based residential treatment.

Outpatient costs are much lower. Treatment is affordable for cash payers, and insurance payers will not quickly exhaust their benefits.

To get the perspective of someone who's been on both sides of this issue and has 14 years of sobriety, I talked to Jeff Dougherty. Jeff is well known in the recovery circles of Orange County, California. He answered my call when I was desperate to find someone to get through to Keven. I had a hunch that he was the kind of person Keven would respect, and I was right. Jeff stopped by the hospital the day after our call to visit Kev. They had a lot in common, and Keven respected Jeff.

Jeff stayed in touch and visited Keven at home. He invited him to celebrate his daughter's birthday—a big bash at a lake. I remember how excited Keven was to be invited, but I wouldn't let him take my car. He'd been using and thought Jeff wouldn't notice. A few days later, Keven was gone. When I spoke with Jeff, he said, "I'll always miss Keven's laugh. I've saved all my text messages from him; he seemed good the last time we talked."

Jeff believes that the entire drug treatment system is broken and needs to be rebuilt from the ground up, using MAT. The current system has many people attending, on average, 10 or more rehab programs. Instead of short-term 30- to 90-day programs, Jeff believes one-year programs are the way to go. During that year, each person deals with the real cause of the drug use—all while working a job, saving money and learning life skills. After that year, they're equipped to start a new life with a strong foundation.

I asked Jeff what he thinks we can do to prevent kids from starting to use drugs in the first place. His answer didn't surprise me:

"Nothing. There is nothing we can do because these kids don't want to feel. They will use fentanyl, knowing it killed two of their friends, because it helps them avoid the feelings of isolation they have."

My heart sank at these words. While I can make suggestions for parents to help their kids steer clear of drugs, there are no guarantees. No family is immune, and like Keven, one time may be all it takes for someone to become dependent.

Jeff said that we live in a society where people feel alone. He thinks isolation is the biggest risk factor for today's youth. Keven certainly struggled with isolation and loneliness. His entire life, he craved a feeling of belonging, to be a part of something bigger than himself. The closest he came to finding it was in the gang affiliates he met in prison because they were a tight group both inside and outside those prison walls.

In Keven's mind, he was unable to find belonging because he didn't think he had value or that anyone understood him. Keven believed that for someone to like him and want to be around him, he'd have to give them something. He didn't feel like he was enough on his own. When he had money, he'd take people out to eat. When someone admired something of his, he often gave it to them. I saw this from the time Keven was a child, and we talked about it often. I couldn't convince my son that people liked him for who he was.

As naïve as this may sound, I stand by my belief that the way we treat substance users makes a big difference in their recovery and is our best hope. A person who feels understood, cared for and accepted is going to have a healthier outlook on life than one who feels looked down upon, dismissed and alone.

When Keven completed rehab the first time, like most

parents, I believed the problem was solved and that life would go back to normal. It was Family Group night, and Therese, my mom and I all attended to support Keven. We sat in a large circle with the clients and their families, and looking around, I saw some were nervous, many were bored and a few were angry.

As each client took their turn sharing, I was shocked to hear how many of them had been through a drug treatment program more than once! My son would only need one time, and then this nightmare would be over. Time is the great teacher.

Keven was only 18 when he attended his first rehab program, and it was a horrible experience for him. He was having panic attacks and passing out, one time hitting his head on the edge of the bathroom sink. The program staff called and asked me to take Keven to an ER—but wasn't he under their care? Shouldn't this facility, which was being paid to support him, be responsible for my son's wellness? My concern was that once Keven was alone with me on the way to the ER he would immediately want to leave rehab and come home. That's exactly what happened. From the moment he got in my car, all through the ER wait and visit, and all the way driving back to the treatment center—he begged me to let him come home. I wouldn't let him. If they called me again to take him to the ER, I would have refused. It was a grueling experience for both of us and caused a lot of unneeded stress. Fortunately, they didn't ask me to take him again.

Exacerbating the complicated rehab rules are co-occurring conditions. Early in Keven's treatment, I learned from one of Keven's doctors that mental illness often goes together with substance use. Keven tried every type of therapy, including Cognitive Behavioral Therapy (CBT), EMDR, Rational Emotive Behavior Therapy and others. He was diagnosed by several psychiatrists with depression, anxiety and panic disorder. Some said he suffered from Bipolar I; others said Bipolar II or OCD, and another thought he had Schizoaffective Disorder. My family started calling me "The Pharmacist" because I studied each medication Keven was prescribed, plus those he wasn't on, to determine what could possibly help and which ones could be detrimental.

If you continue using heroin, meth or other drugs, a mental health diagnosis is impossible, making it difficult to find the right medications. Prescriptions won't work if you're still using, so it's a never-ending cycle of getting nowhere.

Our family would always start out hopeful with a new diagnosis and medication, but Keven hated the way the psych meds made him feel—dull and tired, unable to feel positive or negative emotions. They also caused weight gain and other unpleasant physical side effects. This is why it's so common for people who need this type of help to just quit taking their meds.

One doctor gave Keven a prescription for Klonopin (an anti-anxiety medication similar to Xanax that had a slower absorption rate, so was safer for him to use) because he saw the severity of his anxiety. It was debilitating at times—Keven wouldn't leave the house for a week or two at a time because he only felt safe at home. Usually, Keven would allow me to hold on to his Klonopin so he wouldn't be tempted to take too many at once. This medication is one that can be abused, but it helped Keven get to a level where he could function if he took it as prescribed.

Sometimes Keven combined it with heroin, so it became useless. This would land him back in a treatment facility where drugs that are used to treat anxiety are considered addictive, so they aren't permitted. In my family's years of working with rehab after rehab, doctors, medical professionals and therapists trying to get Keven's co-occurring mental health and substance use issues understood and properly diagnosed and treated, I eventually lost my son. I believe we need a total overhaul in our approach to treating the whole patient.

Today there is a new killer on the streets: fentanyl. This synthetic opioid killed more than 75,000 people between April 2020 and April 2021, according to the CDC's National Center for Health Statistics. Through a Facebook group I follow, "The

Fentanyl Awareness Coalition," I've noticed that a majority of these victims are young, and many are not substance abusers—they are kids that take a pill they believe is a Xanax or ecstasy that is instead laced with a deadly amount of the drug. There are almost 6,000 members of this group, many of whom have lost a loved one to fentanyl. It's a public group, and I urge anyone wishing to increase their awareness about the real and present dangers of street drugs to take a look and read first-hand accounts from families that have been impacted.

An article called "Fentanyl: The Most Dangerous Drug Illegal Drug in America" published in RAND Review on January 13, 2020 paints a harrowing but accurate picture of the fentanyl problem:

> Drug overdoses kill more Americans than car crashes, gunshots, or AIDS at its peak. But it's no longer just a crisis of prescription pills or heroin. It's a crisis of fentanyl. Deaths involving it and other synthetic opioids have surged from around 3,000 in 2013 to more than 30,000 in 2018.
>
> Fentanyl is unlike any other drug problem in modern history. It's more useful to think of it as a mass poisoning than as a traditional drug epidemic. The crisis is likely to get worse. Fentanyl and other synthetic opioids have swept through some parts of the country while leaving others almost untouched. There are signs that's changing.
>
> Confronting the crisis is going to take more than disrupting the supply [chain] and getting people into treatment. Innovative, and controversial, responses—such as supervised drug-consumption sites and fentanyl test strips—must be part of the policy discussion.

CHAPTER 19
UNDERSTANDING THE ADDICTED BRAIN

> The word "addiction'" is derived from a Latin term for "enslaved by" or "bound to." Anyone who has struggled to overcome an addiction—or has tried to help someone else to do so—understands why. Addiction exerts a long and powerful influence on the brain that manifests in three distinct ways: craving for the object of addiction, loss of control over its use, and continuing involvement with it despite adverse consequences.
>
> ~Harvard Health, *Overcoming Addiction: Paths Toward Recovery*

Science shows us that Substance Use Disorder changes the way the brain works. There's a part of the brain called "the reward system." This is where we get the natural "reward" chemical of dopamine released in our brain after we enjoy something we like—hanging out with friends, eating chocolate, making love, going for a run or seeing a comedy show. Drug and alcohol use also causes the brain to release dopamine. For the substance user, certain triggers can also get the dopamine flowing, like thinking about getting high, seeing a friend you get high with, a specific scent or hearing a sound or phrase that reminds you of getting high.

The problem is that when you're using drugs, your brain releases a flood of dopamine—way more than would be released under the normal conditions that make you happy—like from eating a favorite meal or playing your favorite sport. When the drug-induced flood of dopamine saturates your brain, your brain attempts to self-correct by cutting back on natural dopamine production.

As you continue to use drugs, your body produces less and less natural dopamine. Things that used to bring you pleasure no longer produce it, so you lose interest in those old favorite activities and instead crave more drugs to manufacture enough of the feeling just to feel normal. I've heard many substance users say that they enjoy the euphoria of using heroin even more than what they experience when their brains naturally release the pleasure chemicals during sex.

Research also shows how substance use changes the areas of the brain that control judgment, decision making, learning, memory and behavior regulation. Those drug-induced chemical changes to the brain are what lead a star athlete to lose their scholarship after being prescribed opiates for an injury, cause a mother to get a DUI while her kids are in the car or an otherwise shy young woman turning to prostitution to support her drug use.

Willpower changes with SUD. If you try to quit using, your brain tries to protect you from the pain and intensity of withdrawal symptoms. Your brain tells you to do *whatever it takes* to stop the cravings and discomfort. Unless you've been around someone with SUD, it's hard to imagine what a powerful pull this can have. Keven once told me to watch *Requiem for a Dream* to understand him better. Certain scenes from that movie are embedded in my mind and make me feel sick every time I remember them. The movie is not for the faint of heart, but it does get the message across.

Keven went to rehab with gang members, lawyers, homeless people, college grads and high school dropouts, executives, nurses and the average kid next door. SUD doesn't play favorites; it doesn't care about your income, your status, your sexual orientation or your race. But research has shown there are a few factors that do play a role in developing SUD.

- **Genetics**: SUD runs in the family, so you have up to a 60 percent greater risk of becoming a substance user if a family member has the disease.
- **Environment**: Growing up in a home with adults who use drugs increases the risk of substance use and SUD.
- **Development**: Between the teen years and age 25, the brain is still developing. Using drugs during this time increases your chances of long-term substance use and SUD, which can cause serious, irreparable damage.
- **Childhood Trauma**: According to a renowned expert in mind and body health, early childhood development and substance abuse, Dr. Gabor Maté, the cause of SUD is not found in genetics but in the early childhood environment. "Not all addictions are rooted in abuse or trauma, but I do believe they can all be traced to painful experience," Maté wrote in his 2010 bestseller, *In the Realm of Hungry Ghosts: Close Encounters with Addiction*. "A hurt is at the center of all addictive behaviors. It is present in the gambler, the Internet addict, the compulsive shopper and the workaholic. The wound may not be as deep and the ache not as excruciating, and it may even be entirely hidden—but it's there."

Perhaps the most painful part of SUD and recovery is relapse. We shouldn't be surprised when it happens, and it shouldn't involve punishment (like getting kicked out of rehab). The cycle of recovery and relapse can be endless and can lead to death. One relapse can kill you. When someone comes out of recovery and hasn't used drugs for a period of time, environmental triggers can lead substance users to think they can use "differently" this time. Inevitably, they miscalculate their tolerance level, end up using the same amount they used in the past and unintentionally overdose. Since relapse is a common part of a person's recovery journey, it should be included in all discussions about Substance Use Disorder. As Melissa A. Herman and Marisa Roberto stated in their article in *The US National Library of Medicine National Institutes of Health* (March 19, 2015), "Drug addiction is defined as a chronic relapsing disorder that is comprised of three stages: preoccupation/anticipation, binge/intoxication, and withdrawal/negative affect."

I also spoke with two individuals about their experience with SUD and relapse. They both chose to remain anonymous but gave me permission to share their stories.

 All the progress I made in the year and a half I had clean is gone. I'm throwing away everything I worked for. I've been using again for about the last month and a half. I've lost four friends around me in the last month to overdoses. It's funeral after funeral. My four-year relationship is falling apart. I don't want to get out of bed in the mornings anymore. I'm terrified of being sick. I feel like quitting my job because I'm struggling to get through shifts without using. Drugs are all I think about. I've lost my fight, and I don't know how to get it back. I just feel like giving up; no one close to me understands what I'm going through. I feel like I've let everyone down, especially my family. They would be heartbroken if they knew I was using again. I have no one I can talk to about my addiction. Two days ago, my friend almost died on my kitchen floor from an overdose, and we spent 10 minutes doing chest compressions on him until paramedics got to us because he'd stopped breathing. It was so traumatic after being away from that life for so long. I

*don't want this anymore, but I don't know how to stop
again.*

~John

*After five years, I'm using again. My family is devas-
tated; my new friends don't know, so I avoid them. I hate
myself. I hate fucking heroin. I hate how I look when I'm
using—like I'm sneaking around all the time and can't
be trusted. Ha—because it's true! I'm too old for this. I
stay high as much as I can, so I don't have to think about
how to stop. It's only been a few weeks, but it feels like
months. It just grabbed me, man. I just had to do it
again. It came out of nowhere. Or maybe it never really
left—five years of building my life up only to have it
crash. Picking up the pieces sounds impossible; it really
does.*

~Jane

I saw the effects of relapses in Keven and believed him when
he told me how desperately he wanted to quit, but no matter
how hard he tried, he would always fail. One of the last things
he said to me was, "I hate drugs more than anything, but I can't
stop using them and never will be able to." Keven gave up the
battle after fighting for years. Others never give up and are still
here to talk about it.

The statistics of loss to SUD are staggering. According to the
National Institute on Drugs (March 19, 2021), "In 2019, nearly
50,000 people in the United States died from opioid-involved
overdoses. The misuse of and addiction to opioids—
including prescription pain relievers, heroin, and synthetic
opioids such as fentanyl—is a serious national crisis that affects
public health as well as social and economic welfare. The
Centers for Disease Control and Prevention estimates that the
total 'economic burden' of prescription opioid misuse alone in
the United States is $78.5 billion a year, including the costs of

healthcare, lost productivity, addiction treatment, and criminal justice involvement."

Research and study are important and vital to us understanding why and how substance users develop SUD, but a wider and better-informed discussion in the mainstream media and in our communities is the only way to bring about change. Judgment based on false perceptions, misunderstanding and misinformation will continue until the average person can see SUD for what it truly is: not weakness and moral failing but a powerful disease that affects every part of a person's life and continues to take the lives of tens of thousands every year in the US alone.

CHAPTER 20
ESCALATING TRAGEDIES

> *Death doesn't scare the addict; it's life they are scared of.*
> ~Anonymous

My phone rang at around 9 pm one evening. From the caller ID, I saw it was Dylan, one of Keven's drug "friends." In my experience, Keven could get very confused about what made a good friend.

"Barbara, I think Keven's in trouble. He's been saying weird shit and then he took off walking."

"What kind of weird shit? And where the hell are you guys? Can't you get him back to where you are?" I was accustomed to having a quiet night disrupted by Keven's drug-induced behavior, but that didn't make it any less annoying.

He hesitated. It was becoming obvious that this was serious, otherwise he wouldn't have called.

"He's acting really paranoid and thinks the cops are after him. I think he used meth. He was headed down toward the freeway in Irvine."

I thanked Dylan and called Keven. Trying to sound casual I asked, "Hey hon, when are you coming home?" The background noise told me that he was near a busy street.

"Mom, come and get me right now. I've been hiding in the bushes because there's a cop following me." He sounded scared.

"Okay honey, I'll be right there. Tell me where you are." My body went into rescue mode: the now-familiar, sick-anxious feeling flooded my stomach, my heart beat too fast and my breath was hard to catch. Keven gave me a vague idea of where he was, so I went on the hunt. It took me over an hour to finally locate him.

My car pulled up to the curb and he dove into the backseat, lying down so no one could see him. "Mom, we can't go home! They're after me! I'm serious, this is not good!"

How many times can a heart be ripped apart before it breaks? Seeing him like that was too much for me. But there was no choice; this was our reality. I realized taking him home would keep my mom and sister up all night, and I couldn't do that to them.

The look on his face was pure terror. I held back my tears. He was not being chased. No cops were around. His paranoia was meth-induced, but I knew from experience that trying to convince him that it was all in his mind would end in disaster, and he'd run away and go who-knows-where.

I was calm. "Okay, Kev, do you want me to get a hotel room for us tonight?"

"Thank you, Mom, thank you! Yes, please get one." He relaxed into the seat, relieved.

Meth, in my opinion, is far more damaging than heroin. While heroin is statistically more deadly due to the risk of acci-dental overdose, meth causes serious psychotic episodes and can do permanent brain damage because it is made with toxic chemi-cals like battery acid, drain cleaner and antifreeze. Even though he didn't admit to using it because he knew I hated it, Keven couldn't hide the sores on his face, arms or legs from picking at his skin.

As I pulled into the parking lot of a Hampton Inn, I made Keven promise to stay in the car. When the man helping me secure a room looked over my shoulder with a horrified expression, I knew that Keven hadn't done as I asked.

"That's my son, he's with me." *Please just give us the room,* I thought. He handed over the key and I let out a sigh of relief.

Keven needed my company on cigarette breaks outside every 15 minutes. He was convinced every person he saw was out to kill him. To kill time, we got in the car and drove around for a half hour before returning to our room. The entire drive, Keven was peeking out the window saying we were being followed. "Take a quick right Mom, we have to lose them."

Eventually, after a long night spent trying to convince him that he was safe, I finally fell asleep for a few hours. When daylight broke, I opened my eyes to find that Keven had moved every piece of furniture in front of the door. He even tried to pull the refrigerator away from the wall in his desperation to feel safe. Everything in my purse, his pockets and around the room was strewn about. He was hunkered down behind the wall of furniture wearing only his boxers and sweating profusely.

"I can't do this anymore, Mom. I need help. I want to stop using more than anything."

I called work and used a sick day, then spent the rest of the day calling rehabs and driving him to different hospitals and facilities trying to get him help. We were turned away each time. It's impossible to get psychiatric help if the patient has drugs in their system. On the flip side, drug rehabs wouldn't take him because he was "psychotic." I had no choice but to take him home.

I hoped he would be tired enough to fall asleep and then come down from the meth while he was out. If he stayed awake, he would probably damage our house. When he was in this state, he would take a knife or some other sharp object and start carving wooden pieces of our furniture or carving designs into the walls while we slept. He'd also rummage through drawers and cabinets, emptying their contents on the floor. He had no idea he was doing anything wrong; when he did get back to "normal," he would be remorseful and feel bad for causing us stress, damaging the house and making a mess.

These were times when I felt like I couldn't go on. Besides the mental anguish and the emotional rollercoaster, there was also physical exhaustion. Family and friends wondered from the outside how I could keep up with it all, or suggested that I was crazy to put up with it. I loved my son. If I didn't do all I could to help him, who would? I'd never forgive myself if the worst happened and I lost him without trying everything in my power to find him the right treatment. As parents, we do what we have to do. Unfortunately, one symptom of SUD is that it's progressive. It gets worse over time when the user can't get high enough using the normal amount, and they need more and more to get the high they're looking for. As his drug use progressed, his choices worsened and their effects led him down his final road to death.

Keven had been staying at a rehab in Riverside but was kicked out for using. Rather than putting him on the street, they had admitted him into a detox facility associated with their treatment center. I was so happy to know he was somewhere safe.

A few days later, he called to tell me he left the detox with an older woman he had met named Dawn. She had money and got them a hotel room. Even though Dawn didn't use heroin, she was an alcoholic and a diabetic. During their stay together, Keven had to call 911 to have her rushed to the hospital because he couldn't wake her up. She was admitted and then released once her blood sugars were stable.

The following morning at 7 am, Keven called again.

"Mom, Dawn is dead. You need to come get me now. Hurry."

Upon release from the hospital, Dawn began drinking again and passed out. This time, Keven was also passed out from using heroin. He woke up next to her dead body. With traffic, it took me two hours to get there. When I arrived, Keven was sitting on the curb talking to the police. He wasn't in handcuffs, which was a good sign. I glanced in the motel room and saw a woman with long dark hair lying on the bed.

Keven had called 911 right before calling me, but it was obvious that she was gone. The police ruled him out as a suspect when he showed them paperwork that she had almost died the night before. I wasn't allowed to talk to him, so I waited in my car watching the scene before me. I saw them bring Dawn's body out and wondered how old she was. Did she have family? This was another life tragically gone due to substance use. Another normal day in the life of SUD.

The intense hold drugs and alcohol can have over a person is so strong that they are willing to risk everything to get the high that allows them to keep going (until it doesn't). Eventually Keven was released, and I took him back home. He blamed himself for her death, saying he should have made her stop drinking or stayed up to make sure she was okay. If only he'd been sober himself. I reminded him that he should know better than anyone that you can't stop someone from using their drug of choice if they are determined.

Events like these with Keven were commonplace. Trips to the emergency room blur together, and I can't remember which ones happened at which emergency room or hospital or even during what year. As his drug use progressed, so did his nearness to death. The timer was ticking.

A nurse later called me to say Keven had admitted himself because he was suicidal. When I showed up to the hospital, a group of nurses were standing around talking. They pointed me in Keven's direction, but I didn't need to be told where he was. I could hear loud sobs coming from down the hall.

I pulled back the curtain and stepped into his room. He was curled up in the fetal position crying hysterically. I'd never seen him this upset before. "Mom, Mom!" was all he could say.

Putting my arms around him, I started to cry too. Thankfully, it was a small hospital with no other patients near him. I think the nurses planned it that way, as they didn't appear thrilled to have him under their care. He was just another difficult patient. Just another guy on drugs.

I covered Keven's body with mine and held him as best as I could. I wanted him to feel surrounded by my love and safe in my arms. Why, why was my son so tormented by his own life? Did the drugs cause this or were the drugs the result of feeling this way? If you were mentally ill with severe depression and anxiety, how could you summon the determination to get sober when you could barely function in life?

Keven was admitted to the hospital for another 5150 hold. They assigned social workers who were supposed to follow up with him, but they never did. He was told to find a psychiatrist to prescribe his new medications, but finding a decent one who accepted our insurance was nearly impossible. Substance users can always find the unethical doctors to give them whatever they want, no questions asked—those doctors only ask if the meds are working and prescribe more. Keven could easily get free Xanax which he could then sell for $10 per pill, making $300 that he could then use to buy heroin. These doctors can be found in every city and state all over the country, and only diligent citizens can convince equally conscious lawmakers to put a stop to their practices.

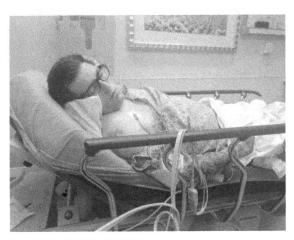

One of Countless Hospital Stays

One evening, Keven was in a dark mood and demanded that I give him money so he could buy drugs. I refused. A few minutes later, I walked into our garage and found him with a maniacal look on his face and the front of his shirt covered with blood. He had stabbed himself in the stomach with a knife.

"Look, I don't care if I live or die!" he said waving the knife around. I begged him to put it down and let me look at his wound. His phone rang. Before I knew what was happening, he had my car keys and was about to drive to Palm Springs, a two-hour drive from our house, to meet his friend who had scored.

"Please, Keven, you'll bleed to death if you drive out there. You need to go to the hospital." He lifted his shirt to show me the wound. It wasn't deep, but it was still bleeding, so he grabbed a nearby towel, jumped in my car and took off.

I received a text a few painful hours later. Keven was fine. There were blood stains on the seats of my car which wouldn't come out. I lived with the reminder of that night until I eventually got a different car.

CHAPTER 21
THE BEGINNING OF THE END

> *Addiction begins with the hope that something "out there'" can instantly fill up the emptiness inside.*
> ~Jean Kilbourne

Gunfire was heard coming from my house. I needed to get home immediately.

"Turn green! Turn green!" I yelled at the traffic light. My next-door neighbor had called to alert me and said she could hear sirens on their way. As I drove toward home, my jaw was clenched, and my hands threatened to break the steering wheel.

Keven was home alone. Shots fired? I ran through all the possibilities: he shot himself. He shot someone else. Someone shot him. He'd been sleeping when I left a few hours ago to run a few errands. How was I suddenly living in a horror movie?

Trying to maintain a safe speed as I drove by the well-manicured yards, I noticed the Orange County Sheriff helicopter circling above. This wasn't the first time they'd been sent on my son's behalf. A few days after his 18th birthday, Keven had swallowed a handful of pills, then disappeared after running out of the house. That time, his girlfriend had alerted me, and I called 911 myself as I made a futile attempt to find him. The helicopter was able to locate him hiding in the bushes at a nearby park just before he passed out. I was certain this time was worse.

Turning the corner onto my street, I saw about 10 police vehicles parked haphazardly and a S.W.A.T. van in front of my house. Some of the officers were already leaving, and the S.W.A.T. guys were taking off their gear and putting it back in their van. This was a good sign, right?

I parked as close as I could get, jumped out of the car and ran toward my house. Keven was sitting on the curb in handcuffs, sweaty and pale. The look on his face reminded me of a young child separated from his parents, waiting for them to come find him at the mall. Handcuffs or no, every cell in my body was relieved to see him alive.

When our eyes met, I watched relief rush over him. He started to talk, but a young officer with bulging biceps covered in tribal tattoos blocked me.

"Ma'am, you can't talk to him. Are you the mother?" I nodded as he led me toward an older officer with gray hair who was slightly less intimidating.

Keven needed me; I could calm him down and reassure him. I wanted to hug him. I understood police procedures, but couldn't they make an exception? Most of these guys knew us from previous incidents over the years. Keven was an adult, but his drug use started in his teens, which left him immature in several ways. He seemed confused and scared.

The older officer explained the situation. "We received a 911 call from your son this afternoon saying six men were in your backyard with their guns pointed at him, and they started shooting. He said he used a shotgun to kill three of them, then ran next door to your neighbor's house with the gun. When your son went to your neighbor's, she called her husband to the door and asked your son for the gun. He handed it over without hesitation. They could hear all the sirens headed this way, so they kept him talking at their house until we got here."

The young officer added, "Your son made it all up except for the part about shooting out the window. He did that. Do you know where he got the shotgun?" I explained that it was an antique that had belonged to my grandfather. The police took the shotgun, a family heirloom. I never got it back.

They asked questions about his mental state and drug use. My answers were hurried because I was distracted by the fact that Keven was so close to me and needed me. He was in a state of psychotic paranoia, probably induced by a drug known as bath salts (a psychoactive stimulant narcotic). Heroin wouldn't cause this; meth might. One prior incident with the police involved Keven calling 911 while standing in the middle of a busy street, surrounded by cops with their guns drawn, threatening to kill him—another hallucination. After that incident, he was not arrested—instead, they took him straight to the hospital.

With the questioning over, I looked at Keven, still on the curb, looking frightened. I pleaded to be allowed to talk to him just for a minute. The young cop said, "No, we can't let you do that," but was cut off by his elder, who said, "Yes, I'll walk you over there, but you can't touch him."

Kneeling on the pavement in front of him, we were at eye level. It was a hot day, and I was wearing shorts. The warm asphalt was digging into my knees. "Listen to me, honey, I know what happened. They are going to take you to jail, but then we'll get you help. It's going to be okay. We'll get through this. We're a team. I love you."

"Okay, Mom, I love you too," he mumbled. I could tell he didn't understand what was going on. This incident was serious, and I knew for a fact he'd do time. Keven was already a convicted felon on probation, so firearms were off-limits. I felt helpless.

I stood up and watched as they pushed Kev into the police car and drove off. He turned and looked at me through the rear window, confused and pleading for help. No matter how many times I saw my son cuffed or in the back of a police car, I never got used to it. Seeing him treated like a criminal rather than someone who needed help filled me with rage that was barely eclipsed by my fear. I'd experienced a lot with Keven over the years—seeing him on life support, visiting him in jail or prison and watching him go through agonizing withdrawal symptoms, but the sight of him in handcuffs was a reminder that he had no control over what was happening in his life.

As the police vehicles left our street, it occurred to me that elementary school kids had been walking home during this ordeal. It must have been scary for some of them. While I had stopped caring about what the neighbors might think every time we had an incident, this was different. The neighbors had every right to be upset. I shuddered to think about what could have happened.

Not everyone has experienced the family disease of SUD, so it's not uncommon for some to pass judgment with no under-standing. I knew who my son was, and I was proud of him. They could judge and gossip all they wanted. I've never been ashamed of my son. Never.

Kev was not his actions, and he was not his substance use or his mental illness. There was shame in some choices he made, but that was the drugs claiming victory over his true nature. He made the poor choice of trying heroin at age 17, not knowing it would change the course of his life. Inside he was still a quality person and my loving son.

I felt I owed the neighbors an explanation, and I wanted the truth gossiped about rather than rumors. I wrote a letter to each of them, assuring them that their children could feel safe playing and walking on our street. I did my best to educate them about drug use without coming across as defensive. A few neighbors thanked me, but for the most part, I didn't receive feedback.

That night I waited for Keven's call from jail, but it never came. I didn't hear from him until the next evening.

"Mom, why am I here?'" Keven's voice was shaky and quiet. He was on the verge of panic and in the early stages of with-drawal. He had no recollection of the events that landed him at the Men's Central Jail in Santa Ana. I asked him what drugs he was on when it happened, but he didn't want to answer the question (probably because he knew our conversation was being recorded). But silence can speak volumes between two people who know each other very well.

CHAPTER 22
PRISON F'D HIM UP

> The prison environment is almost diabolically conceived
> to force the offender to experience the pangs of what
> many psychiatrists would describe as mental illness.
> Incarceration can cause lasting damage to mental health.
>
> ~Dr. Seymour L. Halleck, *Research Roundup:
> Incarceration Can Cause Lasting Damage to Mental
> Health*

The differences between prison and jail are huge. Jail is where they take you after you're arrested. The Sixth Amendment of the U.S. Constitution states that you "have the right to a speedy and public trial." So, within 48 hours of Keven being arrested for possession of a firearm and breaking his parole, he was standing before a judge.

Sometimes an attorney or public defender will tell you to give up this right. They do this so they'll have enough time to look at the facts of your case and determine how long it will take to prepare for trial. It's also common knowledge among lawyers that the older a case gets, the more likely it will be resolved in favor of the defendant. Either way, there will be some time waiting in jail for your case to be resolved unless you have someone to bail you out.

Prison is where you go once a sentence for a year or more has been set. Lesser sentences can sometimes be served in the county jail, especially due to prison overcrowding in California. Even long sentences are sometimes served in jail, depending on the severity of the crime.

Prison has its pros and cons, as I learned from Anthony, Keven and others. Somehow in prison, you have more freedom than you have in jail. You get "yard," which means you get to be outdoors where you can work out, walk or play basketball for up to an hour a day. You also get "contact visits" that last for several hours. These are preferred because two adults can visit at once, and you can sit across the table from your loved ones.

Serving your time in prison also means you can receive "quarterly packages," where items can be shipped from a third party as approved by the prisons. Typically, the incarcerated person will send an order form, and the order is placed online. Basics like socks and new shoes, coffee, snacks and hygiene items are approved and ship directly from the vendor.

With all its advantages over jail, going to prison is far more dangerous. For survival, almost every incarcerated person is eventually approached by a gang to affiliate (typically based solely on race) so they can protect you. You may be serving time for drugs and still be around violent people serving life sentences for murder.

When Keven's court case ended, he was sentenced to 16 months in state prison with time served. I attended all of Keven's court dates, and on this day, Anthony also had a court appearance in the same courtroom. We chose a seat that would allow us to see Keven, who was seated inside the "glass cage." He wasn't allowed to wave or acknowledge us in any way, but that didn't stop him from smiling at us and making the occasional eye roll when the bailiff wasn't watching. When it was time to leave, Anthony put his hands together to form a heart, pointed at himself and then at Keven: "I love you." It was the last time they would see each other because, within six months, Anthony would be dead.

For years I'd been attending court proceedings for both boys and had watched hundreds of cases go before various judges. While the system is broken and causes far more harm than good, many of the judges are good and fair. Substance users and the mentally ill are treated like criminals and sent to prison, which typically ruins their lives. It might be called the "California Department of Corrections and Rehabilitation," but shamefully, until very recently, there has been very little rehabilitation going on.

A convicted felon's future is as bleak as if they were still in prison. The label of "felon" comes with the stigma of being an outcast in society, considered untrustworthy and irredeemable. There are, of course, exceptions—I know several young men who were released, got jobs and have created satisfying and beautiful lives for themselves.

The night after Keven received his sentence, he called me from prison. "Mom, it's not as bad as I thought it was going to be. They'll be sending me to Wasco prison for reception soon." He'd expected far worse than 16 months with time served. He'd be home in a little over a year. "I won't be able to call you for three months, but I'll write. Can you be sure there's money on my books, so I can buy coffee and stuff?"

Incarcerated people aren't given much for free. Other than clothes, they receive a bar of soap, a towel, a washcloth and a rolled-up mattress, which they place on a concrete block or the top or bottom bunk in a larger cell. If you were indigent, your package also has hygiene items. I provided money, so Keven could buy himself a pillow, coffee and snacks, deodorant and whatever else he needed to make his stay easier. Even if I believed in the tough love approach, Keven was already being punished.

Not being able to talk to or visit Keven for three months felt like I was being punished, too. I had never gone more than a month without talking to him. While he was at Wasco, we wrote often and had some great conversations, ending every letter with, "I love you more than anything, Keven" and "I love you more than anything, Mom."

Keven did well at Wasco; he read a lot and was committed to turning his life around. He became interested in poetry after reading Billy Corgan's book, *Blinking with Fists*. He read everything by Og Mandino and was learning how to be successful and live a better life. He also read two very popular books that seem to be required reading while in prison: *The Art of War* by Sun Tzu and *The 48 Laws of Power* by Robert Greene.

I sensed a positive change in Keven's willingness to put all his efforts into starting fresh when he got out. I weighed my words with Keven, careful not to lecture him in any way (no one responds well to lectures), so I canned all my pep talks and encouraged him by telling him I was proud. I could see the changes.

I allowed myself to feel encouraged in the moment but didn't hold on to hope too tightly. I knew better—hope was often shattered. There's a saying among parents of substance users: "As long as they're breathing, there's hope." This was supposed to be comforting, but every time I heard it, I felt fearful that Keven's breathing would stop.

One night, Keven called and said, "Mom, I know this will piss you off, but I told them about my preference for prison, and I didn't choose the one close to you. It will be a three-hour drive each way to see me."

I was not pleased to hear this. They let you choose which prison you go to? This didn't sound right to me.

"Well, no. They ask where your family lives because they want to make it convenient for the family to visit. But Norco is the shittiest prison in California. I don't want to get stuck there, so I told them I'd like to be farther north."

I was pissed. I intended to visit often, but if it meant a six-hour round trip, once a month would be all I could manage. In the end, he was sent to Norco, just a 45-minute drive from my house. He was right. It was terrible.

Norco is an incredibly old, run-down facility that was once a luxury hotel in the 1920s. It later served as a Naval hospital, then a narcotics center. Finally, in 1980 they converted it to a medium-security prison. I was so excited to see Kev that I couldn't sleep the night before our first visit.

Preparing for a prison visit starts with planning what to wear and what to bring. The dress code is strictly enforced. If you show up in clothing that violates the code, you are sent to a portable building staffed by volunteers and forced to change into donated clothing.

The only items you could bring into the visiting area were an identification card, one car key, one pack of unopened tissues and cash, which had to be in a clear bag.

My mother had passed away six months earlier, and I was glad she didn't have to see Kev in that environment. Both Keven and I lived with a lot of guilt for all we put her through, but she never stopped loving him and believing in him. She would have been especially hurt to see how dark Keven's life became after prison.

Therese went with me on the first visit. I'd been to two other prisons before, so I had a good idea of what to expect. As we drove through the neighborhood of Norco, we noticed it was a "horse town." The prison felt out of place. We pulled up to the entrance, and to our right was a huge sports field where kids were playing soccer. The sound of refs blowing their whistles and parents cheering for their kids filled the air. Straight across the street stood looming towers with armed guards and miles of fences topped with wicked-looking barbed wire. Each of the convicted felons imprisoned inside those walls was once a little boy that may have run around on a soccer field or a baseball diamond like the one right there. I wondered if they could hear the kids playing, remembering when they were once carefree and full of hope. Or maybe it tortured them, reminding them that they were missing out on the lives of their kids.

The parking lot was made of dirt and chunks of ancient asphalt. At the front of the lot were some shaded benches—the first waiting area. I was grateful for the shade because, typically, visitors could spend hours standing in the sun, waiting to visit an inmate. The waiting period can be anywhere from an hour to a few hours, so just like prisoners passing the time, visitors are forced to cultivate patience.

After filling out the "visitor slip," I joined Therese on a bench. Children were running around laughing, waiting to visit their dads. I thought back to Keven's childhood, wondering about what our lives would be like today if I did a few things differently. Would I still be sitting here, waiting to see my boy in prison?

After about 45 minutes, it was time for our group to enter. We transferred to a new bench, where we removed our shoes for the officer to inspect. Next was the metal detecting wand waved over our bodies, front and back. Then we formed a line and waited another 10 minutes for a metal gate to open for our group. We crammed ourselves into the small space, and the gate closed behind us. For a few moments, we were all trapped together inside this little cage, pushed up against strangers. We all had the same thing in common: someone we loved was inside. The guard in the tower opened the gate on the opposite side that led into the indoor waiting area.

Once inside the next waiting room, we dropped our visitor slips in a box and waited for our names to be called, then formed another line to show our ID and have our hands stamped. Then we could walk across the yard and into the huge portable building, the "visiting center," which was filled with orange and blue plastic tables and chairs, the walls lined with vending machines. The tables were very short and looked like they belonged in a kindergarten class. It was designed like this intentionally so that visitors couldn't hide their hands, pass contraband or hold hands with the person they'd come to visit. Again, we stood in line, this time to be assigned a table number. We'd been there for two hours at this point.

Once we made it to the final and most intense waiting period, Therese and I sat at our little table, straining our necks to see the line forming at the other end of the room. All the blue prison uniforms were identical, but when I saw Keven's sun-starved, pale face peeking out, my heart was dancing, and my stomach was doing somersaults. I had never felt so happy and nervous at the same time. He walked into the room with a solemn expression, attempting to look tough. When he spotted us, he couldn't help but grin. We were allowed a three-second hug, and as I held him in my arms for that moment, I was tempted to grab him and make a run for it. Instead, I gave my sister her turn.

We spoke at least three times a week, so there wasn't anything new to talk about. After our initial hellos, he asked if I'd get him some long-awaited snacks. Incarcerated people look forward to having the treats offered by the vending machines that are stocked with both hot and cold foods, with a row of microwaves available. The line for the microwave was the worst; people had little patience awaiting their turn to warm up food. It was chaotic, and once again, I was packed in with a crowd of people. Only visitors were allowed to use the machines, so the people being visited had to stand in the back of the crowd yelling, "Pizza!" and "Popcorn!" at them. Keven asked for cinnamon rolls, candy and a breakfast burrito.

Looking around the room, I noticed the men with their children. These big tough guys were immediately gentle and affectionate with their kids. Some of the women looked deeply in love with their men, while others looked like they couldn't wait to leave. Occasionally, someone would walk by and acknowledge Keven by lifting his chin.

"Is that one of your friends?" I asked.

"You don't have friends here, Mom! Some people are cool, but you must keep your guard up constantly; you never know for sure who you're dealing with." Keven and Anthony had been in jail together a few times but not in the same area; they'd only see each other at chow hall.

Therese, Kev and I were all making an effort to keep the conversation going. Keven asked about each of the pets one at a time. I asked him what a typical day was like. That took up about five minutes. Our long-awaited visit was awkward, and we left feeling empty after our two hours. Little did I know that would be the best visit we'd have during Keven's stay at Norco.

"What's Anthony up to, Mom?" I didn't have the heart to tell Keven that he was at my house almost every day. I knew that would make him jealous. He saw how close Anthony and I were, and even though he had begged me to give Anthony a chance, sometimes he resented our relationship.

Keven asked for news on what all of his friends were up to. He asked about the yard and the koi pond, something he cared about. Small talk faded into an actual conversation. "I hate it here, Mom. It's not like Wasco." He reminded me how things inside a prison are run more by the gangs than the guards. "Mom, I had to affiliate with the Whites, but there's only three of us in our dorm, so the Mexicans are the ones calling the shots."

I understood what he meant. I had done my research and learned that you don't have to affiliate with a gang (affiliation is not the same as joining, it's more like siding with that group). But if you didn't, no one had your back, and you were more vulnerable to being preyed upon. Keven had always been more of a follower than a leader, so I wasn't surprised that he affiliated himself with the white guys. Prison is divided by race, with the whites affiliated with the Aryan Brotherhood or the Nazi Lowriders, Black people with the Black Guerrilla Family and Hispanics with either the Mexican Mafia or the Nuestra Family. If you were Asian or of mixed race, you had to choose which one fit you best. Keven had no gang ties but believed the only way to stay safe in prison was to affiliate.

His entire life, Keven wanted to "belong" to some type of

brotherhood or group where people looked out for each other and were loyal and committed to one another. It was a long-running theme throughout his life. He never joined a gang, but he hung out with some gang members when he got out and seemed proud that they allowed him into their lives. He had been a Boy Scout and had a group of friends at church—he even tried to join the Masons—but nothing filled his need for belonging. He'd been let down too many times, so after prison, he believed he finally found some "solid guys" that would have his back and vice versa.

"Honey, just be careful here. I don't want you getting hurt or getting in more trouble. I'll make sure you have books to read and money on your books to buy coffee and snacks."

"Thanks, Mom, that helps." It was all I could do from the outside other than writing encouraging letters and visiting every other week on his allotted visit day.

When it was time to leave that day, it was almost impossible to hold back the tears, and I knew Keven could see my eyes turning red. My son was stuck in a terrible environment with no one who cared about him. We hugged, and Therese and I watched Keven walk back through the cramped room to the area where they re-cuffed him and sent him to his barracks. I sobbed all the way home, drained and already missing Keven—already dreading the next depressing visit.

I never missed a chance to see Keven. I accepted every phone call, and I responded to every letter. But I didn't want to most of the time. As the months wore on, Keven became demanding and rude. He was often in a foul mood. He'd write to apologize for being distant during a visit or mean on a phone call. I dreaded talking with him because it was typically negative and depressing.

Then came the visit from hell. As Keven approached me, I noticed his hands were covered with tattoos that had not been there the previous visit. "Not your hands!" I screamed inside my head. I vowed not to make a big deal about it since there was no going back—he'd already done it. But that resolve vanished the second I saw the tattoos up close. The backs of his hand had the faces of two women that looked evil. Across one hand were the numbers "1503," a gang code for Orange County. But those were nothing compared to the large bold letters he had tatted across his fingers: P U R E on one hand and H A T E on the other.

I couldn't control myself: "What the fuck, Keven!" I didn't bother saying hello. Instead, I lectured him on all the reasons this was a terrible decision—it would make it harder to get a job, form terrible first impressions and set a bad example for his children, if he ever had any. On and on I went. It felt like a gut punch; I was so disappointed, angry and worried about that damn message front and center for the world to see. After I purchased his vending machine goodies, I got up and left.

You might wonder how the incarcerated get tattoos in prison. They are creative and can invent just about anything they need. There are common items they purchase for themselves that can be turned into tattoo guns and ink. For ink, they typically use baby oil or Vaseline because it is petroleum-based, and they can burn soot into it, making it ink. Lighters and matches aren't allowed, so a flame is created by opening an electrical socket, then holding a pencil tip and a wire up to the inside. This creates a spark that you can use to make into a flame by holding a piece of paper or tissue against the spark until it catches. To make the tattoo gun, you need a rotary motor, a mechanical or Bic pen, a teaspoon or toothbrush, a guitar string, some black electrical tape, scissors, pliers and an electrical socket. Anthony explained all of this to me. He gave a lot of tattoos in prison in exchange for coffee and snacks.

The Guy Who Gave Keven Prison Tattoos

My Favorite of Kev's Tattoos!

Norco prison changed Keven. It broke him and stripped away the last shreds of innocence he possessed. He lived in fear and was forced to do things that went against his nature. Gang violence and criminal activity within prison walls are both common and dangerous. There was plenty of heroin in prison, some brought in by dirty guards wanting the extra money. They would bring in cell phones and all kinds of contraband for money. Since incarcerated people aren't allowed to have money, it was sent from the outside. Drug deals occurred the same way:

you have someone on the outside pay the money to the seller's person on the outside.

One night, Keven called and sounded desperate and scared, but since phone calls are recorded, he couldn't tell me why. "Mom, come visit this weekend. I need to talk to you."

Once again, the familiar sinking feeling took over my body.

"Something happened, and I need you to be okay with it." I knew better than to ask what, so I reassured him and found myself tense with anxiety for the rest of the week. When Keven was locked up, there was peace in the house. I slept better knowing where he was. But after this next visit, all that went to hell, and I got back on the worry train, taking side trips to anger and hopelessness.

I arrived early to see Keven that day. I could tell from across the room that something was not right. As he got closer, I saw he had been beaten up. Knowing that reacting to this in public would be an enormous embarrassment to him, I kept calm.

His eyes were darting around the room, and I noticed he had a black eye and a cut on his cheek. He didn't ask me to rush over to the vending machine. "I'm in trouble, Mom. I did something stupid, and I need your help. A few weeks ago, this guy brought in some heroin. I knew I could get some, but I didn't ask. I swear to God, Mom, I didn't want to do it."

My facial expression was understanding, and I urged him to go on. Inside felt like a bomb had detonated in my gut and exploded out the top of my head.

"Well, the main guy, he offered me some for free." The dealers immediately sensed that Keven was an easy mark, the perfect pawn for their illegal activities.

Keven had over 10 months sober, four awaiting his trial in jail, three from Wasco and three from his first months here at Norco. This was the longest stretch of sobriety in his life. He had three more months there! Looking back, I should have received an acting award for always being the calm mom on the outside. "Go on, what happened to you?"

"Well, he offered it to me again a few days later and said I didn't have to pay again. I kind of knew something bad would happen, but I used again. The next day he told me I needed to do him a favor." Keven was still talking with his eyes darting around the room. Was he looking for someone or avoiding looking at me? "Mom, they made me knife a guy. Not stab him, but cut him across the face deep enough to leave a scar."

Keven was many things, but violent wasn't one of them. Sure, he and Anthony had some stories about beating up drug dealers, but it was likely that Anthony was doing the hitting, and I didn't even know if the stories were true or not. I tended to think most of the stories were exaggerated.

"I hated doing it," he continued. "I didn't want to—it was this young Mexican kid. So, the next day they gave me more heroin, and I didn't even try to say no—I wanted it. But now they want money. Mom, you have to get it to them, or things will be dangerous for me in here." He explained that they threatened to scar his face like he did to the kid, then they beat him up to give him a taste of what would happen if he couldn't come up with the money. I buried my face in my hands, trying so hard not to cry. I was defeated.

If I agreed, it would go on and on until he got out. But what if I didn't give him the money? The same thing had happened with Anthony once, and I had said no. He got beat up so badly that he had to transfer to protective custody and be housed with convicted child molesters.

I told Keven I'd think about it, but he insisted I tell him right there. So I said yes, I would pay his debt off this one time but never again—famous last words.

For the next three months, I cringed every time my phone rang and I saw the familiar phone number pop up. I had no money. I was making enough to get by paycheck to paycheck, but that was it. I ended up selling things I had planned on owning forever. Any item of value was taken to a pawn shop or a gold exchange store. I lived in fear of someone showing up at my house to ask me for money in person. The dealers would request "Green Dot" cards that could be used as cash. I'd mail them to whomever they wanted me to—their wife or their drug connection on the outside. Then they wanted cash only. I worried my bank would somehow know why I was getting cash out and getting advances on all my credit cards.

One afternoon, I ran into a police officer when I was on my daily lunch break walk.

"Officer, can I get your advice on something?"

He looked curious and said, "Sure."

I told him the whole story about the drugs in prison and me paying the dealers on the outside. "Officer, what can I do to put an end to this? I'm not only broke, I'm in serious debt from this."

He shook his head and said, "There's nothing you can do from a legal standpoint unless you want to put your son's life in danger. It's your call: you can keep paying or stop and let your son suffer the consequences."

"What would you do if it were your son?" I asked.

He looked up for a minute, contemplating. "I'd keep paying."

By the time Keven was ready to be released, our relationship was at odds, and he had a full-blown heroin problem again. At one time, I marked my calendar in anticipation of him coming home. Now I was filled with dread.

On the day I picked Keven up, he was silent. Other than a few words when he got in the car, he had nothing to say to me on the 45-minute ride home. I was depressed and upset. He was haunted by some things he'd done in there and wanted his next fix. The next day he told me he'd get back on Suboxone, and I was elated! I made an appointment with his SUD specialist.

Dr. Smith put Keven on Suboxone, and even though we all had the best of intentions, Keven's drug use started progressing again.

CHAPTER 23
MY BEAUTIFUL BOY

> *The heart of a mother is a deep abyss at the bottom of which you will always find forgiveness.*
> ~Honoré de Balzac

August 11, 2020 was a hot summer day in Southern California. Like every morning, I began my day, sitting in my serene backyard, enjoying my coffee. Keven and I had just ended a familiar conversation about how much he hated drugs but could not stop using them. He'd been trying to stop for 13 years but, at this point, could only ever string together a few months of sobriety here and there. His goal was to have his life together by age 30, which was rapidly approaching. I reminded him he only had to get through this moment, then the next. One moment, one hour and one day at a time.

Keven didn't like being touched, but that morning he allowed me to put my arms around him and hug him. He wasn't wearing a shirt, so I sensed his skin against mine and recall appreciating such a special moment since it was so rare. If only I had known it would be the last time I felt his heartbeat against mine.

Just 15 minutes later, the sound of a gunshot reverberated through my home. Dashing up the stairs to his room, my chest felt like it was going to cave in; it was hard to breathe. It seemed like I was swimming against a riptide, not able to get to Keven's room fast enough. I couldn't survive if Keven was gone—it would be the end of my life too.

I found my son lying across his bed with a 9 mm gunshot wound above his right temple. My only child was gone. Forever. I was frozen, waiting for my brain to process what my eyes were seeing. A fountain of blood was shooting straight up in the air from the hole in his head. Time stopped. The heavy, hot air created a blanket of stillness on the room. I waded through the empty space between us and touched his wrist. It was warm. There was no pulse. He was dead. My son was dead.

Someone screamed. From miles away, I heard, "No, no!" It was me. I was outside of my own body, peering over my own shoulder. Therese was there now, shouting his name through her own sobs. My mind and body were at war; my brain was in crisis mode, ready to call 911, but my body wouldn't leave Keven's side. I might miss a second of his fading warmth. I wanted to hold him so tight that his life stayed inside him—give my life for his.

Eventually, the spell broke, and my body went into action. Out of pure instinct, I used a towel to try stopping the bleeding, knowing he was already gone. I ran back downstairs to find my phone. When the 911 dispatcher answered, I was hysterical but told her through tight breaths, "My son—shot himself. He's —dead!"

"Have you tried CPR?" she asked. She didn't understand that it was too late. I had been trying CPR on Keven for 13 years.

"No! My son is dead. He shot himself in the head. He's dead. He's gone!" I explained that I'd checked for a pulse. His body was still warm but lifeless. She directed my sister and me to wait outside for the officers to arrive, and I followed her directions, grateful to have someone tell me what to do. There is no instruction manual for mothers when they find their dead child.

But leaving the house meant that when the police arrived, I

wasn't allowed back into Keven's room. I needed more time with him. I wish I had stayed next to him, stroking his arm like I always did when he was going through a hard time. I wish I had a few more maternal moments with my son before they took his body away from me forever.

Ross's mom, Anyce, had heard the gunshot and my screaming and came running. Her own tears mixed with mine as she held me. I was so grateful to have someone with me who had known my boy since childhood. She'd watched his tragic struggles for years and was one of the few who knew the real Keven.

The other neighbors gathered across the street and watched what was happening. Keven didn't have the best reputation in our neighborhood, so even though they had lived near our family for decades, only one neighbor sent me their condolences afterward.

When a suicide occurs, officials consider it a crime scene until the investigation is complete. We were forbidden to enter our home, so we sat on the front porch, sobbing, with the sun glaring down on us. I tried to forget my last sight of Keven, lying on his bed with a gaping hole above his right temple. I didn't have to wonder why Keven had taken his life. He did it because he was done. He'd fought the war and lost. He was too exhausted and tormented to go on. Hope and determination had vanished, and he believed this was the only way to find peace. He had been killing himself slowly for 13 years.

The moment Keven's finger pulled the trigger, my life was forever changed. I lost the person who defined me, the person who taught me what love was, who gave me purpose. How could I live without my precious son? Why would I want to? Who am I if I am not Keven's mom?

Deep within my mind, I could hear him whispering to me, "It's okay, Mom. I wouldn't have done it if I didn't think you could handle it."

Therese sat on the bench on our front porch and I sat on the ground in front of the door. The sun was right in our eyes. We sobbed until our eyes were swollen shut and our throats were dry as gravel from screaming. I asked an officer for water, and he yelled at our audience gathered across the street, "Can one of you bring them water?" A neighbor I didn't recognize brought over two bottles.

"Officer, can we please move to the backyard?" I wanted some privacy and to get out of the heat. The officer allowed it, but he kept close guard on us for hours. He correctly sensed that I would have run upstairs to be with Keven if given an opportunity.

A volunteer from the Traumatic Intervention Program (TIP) arrived. This nonprofit organization provides emotional aid and practical support to victims of traumatic events in the first few hours following a tragedy. Years earlier, I had signed up to take the course to become a volunteer for them, but when Keven started using drugs, I dropped out—my daily life had so much trauma and drama that I didn't have anything left to give to others.

The volunteer was kind and supportive and filled us in on what to expect at every stage. Just having her sitting there with us as a witness to our grief brought comfort. She acknowledged that we were experiencing the worst moments of our lives.

Eventually, the coroner finished her exam and told me they would be taking Keven's body. Next to her stood the deputy coroner who said, "Suicide is a selfish thing to do." I couldn't argue, so I just shook my head. Suicide is a last resort for the mentally ill and unstable who are trying to survive an unbearable existence.

I'd waited an eternity to see Keven one last time before they took him from me, so I was devastated when they wouldn't let me see him. The officials brought him down the stairs in a body bag, discreetly covered with a navy-blue blanket. One of the men carrying him suggested I let our dog say goodbye to him. I held Sugar up and let her sniff; then, I followed them out the door and down the driveway to the coroner's van.

Keven's foot was uncovered inside the opaque body bag. I grasped his foot in desperation, squeezing it and sobbing over my son's body until they told me they needed to close the van door. When they pulled away from my house, I ran after them until they were too far away to see. My legs somehow carried my empty body back home.

The TIP volunteer had arranged a "Traumatic Scene Clean-Up Crew" to take care of Keven's room. They removed all of the bloody items and cleaned up any blood. They removed Kev's bed and everything on it but gave me his watch and bracelets. They took his laptop and his phone because they happened to be on the bed, so I lost access to any pictures or videos I could have had to remember him by. They were thorough, using luminol on the walls, ceiling and floors to be sure to clean every drop of blood.

Downstairs in the living room, the owner of the company, Philip, knelt before my chair and took my hands. I can't recall his exact words, but his condolences and compassion were so sincere they took me by surprise. He told me not to worry about the $5,000 cost as our homeowner's insurance should pay for it. He gave me his number and said I could call him at any time with questions. He genuinely cared about his clients.

When he was gone, the house was a tomb. Therese and I were drowning in the reality of our loss. We tried to find peace by reminding ourselves that Keven was no longer suffering. This helped a bit but didn't take away the anguish of knowing he was gone forever.

Those early days of grief were so heavy that it was difficult to think or move. On the outside, I looked the same, but I felt like a walking, breathing wound, oozing sadness and sorrow. One moment I was sobbing or screaming; the next, I was trying to think about the logistics of burying my son.

I was dating a man named Peter, who lived seven hours

away. When I called him, he knew immediately what had happened and could feel the weight of my grief through the phone. He dropped everything and made the long drive over to support me.

I called Keven's father, who handed the phone to his wife. I think he was speechless. I called my brother, David, who just appeared at some point. I must have called my best friend, Kathy, but I don't remember. She had always offered to drive the six hours between us when Keven and I were in crisis. I'd always told her I didn't need her to come down unless he died. The time had come.

I relied on my family to spread the news to their kids and peripheral friends. But my aunt, a 93-year-old nun, had a special connection with Keven. Whenever I talked to her, she always asked about him and told me how special he was and that he was blessed to have me as a mom. She prayed for him every day and was able to see inside Keven to his troubled soul. Telling her would be the hardest. For once, I was thankful my mother was no longer here, as this would have broken her to pieces. I silently thanked Keven for waiting this long.

David and Keven loved each other but had a strained relationship. My brother saw the hell that Keven put me, our mother and sister through. His support was so valuable for Therese and me. He and Peter took excellent care of Therese and me for the next 10 days, not letting us lift a finger and helping me manage the long list of things I needed to take care of.

Once I shared the news on social media, messages came flooding through. The support networks I had built meant that every understanding message and comment felt like a hug. I needed them all. It also kept me busy, which loosened the grip of anxiety I felt tightening around my heart. I had the constant feeling that I should be doing something. Peter worried that the messages were creating stress because I spent so much time replying to them. But the opposite was true: it helped every agonizing minute pass quicker.

The outpouring of love and concern was so healing. One afternoon before the memorial, four people from my support group came to the house with food and drinks for anyone who might drop by. These friends had all been through the loss of a child from an accidental overdose. While Keven's death wasn't an overdose, the outcome was the same: a broken heart and a lifetime of grief.

The day after Keven died, Peter drove Therese and me to the mortuary. It was quiet in the car. I wasn't in my body—I was watching from somewhere above: a woman in the passenger seat of a car on her way to arrange her son's memorial and cremation.

Standing in the mortuary's meeting room, the coffin and urn samples closed in on me. Because of his obsession with death, Keven had told me exactly what he wanted: an open casket. No suit—he wanted a short-sleeved shirt so his tattoos would show. He wanted my grandfather's rosary around his neck. He wanted to be buried, not cremated. I did my best to honor his wishes but couldn't afford a burial. You can't imagine the cost of dying until you're handed the bill. Kathy had started a GoFundMe account to help with the expenses, and the $7,000 she raised did help. I ended up saving some money by choosing the cardboard coffin and cremation instead of burial. The casket was covered with blue fabric, so even though it was cheap, it wasn't tacky. My Keven deserved a nice casket, but this would have to do.

The funeral director, Rebecca, wanted to know something, but I missed the question. I looked at Therese, and she answered the question. Rebecca gave me a to-do list that included writing the obituary, picking out music and photos for the memorial video and writing some words for the back of Keven's remembrance card. She told me they'd do their best to make him presentable in an open casket.

How is a grieving mom supposed to take care of all this in a matter of days? How do you sum up a life in a few paragraphs? How do you shrink the love of a mother for her son into an hour-long service? Like a robot, I wrote the obituary without too much trouble. It was honest, and it honored Keven. I wrote a poem for the back of the 6 x 4 memorial card. Choosing photos of him was easy—I had a lifetime of pictures to choose from.

Deciding on music was the biggest challenge. Music was a huge part of Keven's life, so I wanted to be thoughtful. I decided on "Sick and Tired" by Iann Dior and Machine Gun Kelly, and for myself, Lynyrd Skynyrd's "Simple Man." It was fitting—a mother's words of wisdom to her only son, encouraging him to take his time, to not live too fast, to find something he loved and to chase the dream instead of money. There was a third song, and believe it or not, I can't remember what it is. I am unable to watch the DVD they gave me with the tribute because I have nothing to play it on. I have a hard time remembering to this day, another symptom of deep grief.

The days leading up to the memorial felt like weeks. I spent time sitting in Keven's room, looking through his things. Some of his friends dropped by, and I let them each pick out something of his as a keepsake. When Ross drove up from Los Angeles, he told me about a heart-to-heart talk they had shared that allowed them to make peace with each other. Keven's friend Matt stopped by with his girlfriend, and when he hugged me, I pretended Keven's arms were around me. They had been in a two-man cell together for months and became very close. Once they were both out, they picked up their friendship again. Matt and I became close, and I appreciated what a good influence he was on Keven.

We held the service at the Mortuary Chapel in the middle of the 2020 COVID-19 pandemic, so we were only allowed 50 people in a room that normally held 270. I was forced to invite people, which was very awkward. I included Keven's four best friends from childhood. I invited his close friend, Matt. Keven's dad, stepmom, half-brother and half-sister were invited. Two of my former co-workers came. A few people from my support group were also there. Kathy had taken a train from central California. We all wore masks and sat a safe, socially-distanced space away from each other.

Peter, Therese and I arrived early. It's not uncommon for people to avoid looking at a dead body, choosing to remember the person as they were in life. But I couldn't wait to see Keven that morning. It gave me comfort knowing I was both honoring his wishes and providing myself with an opportunity to see him one last time. Keven had left his body days before, but the vessel that carried him around all these years was precious to me. The time I got to spend alone with the body I'd given birth to, the body that swam next to me in the ocean, the body that I held in my arms so many times was precious. I loved this flesh—this body—even though it was empty.

As I approached the side of the coffin, my heart was both broken and filled with love. There he was. I leaned over and kissed Keven's cold hard lips, remembering how tiny and sweet his mouth was as an infant. "Keven, I love you more than anything, and I always will. I'm not mad at you; I get it. I understand you held on for as long as you could. You're free now."

My beautiful son—his thick dark lashes closed over blue-green eyes. His face was pale. I chose his favorite short-sleeved, button-down shirt that showed off his arm tattoos like he wanted. I reached in and ran my hands up and down each arm, then caressed his cheek. He wore a hat—his favorite dark gray fedora—and it perfectly covered the bullet entry wound. He wore the only nice watch he hadn't sold. They had carefully covered the bruising around his left eye with make-up. He looked good.

I would never see Keven again. I was savoring each second. Keven looked perfect to me. He didn't look waxy or creepy. He looked like my baby boy at age 29. Before I took my seat, I leaned down and kissed his lips one last time, and instead of his usual scent—a mix of cigarette smoke and Aqua Di Gio—I inhaled the scent of death and decomposition. By the end of the day, Keven would be a pile of ashes in a plastic bag.

The service went well. My family was in the front row on the right, and Jim's family was in the front row on the left. When I saw Jim walking to his seat, I spontaneously ran to him. We shared tears and a long, warm embrace. In a single moment, all the years of tension and resentment melted away.

Keven's friends shared some crazy stories that brought some much-needed laughter to the room. My former boss, Clyde, spoke as well—and though I don't remember what he said, I know I felt that his words were perfect.

In addition to Keven's friends and family, there were three women from Solace. Maggie, the founder, spoke. I was surprised to see that Pastor Lyle from the church I'd attended for years was there. He had lost his first wife to suicide. I remember every face that showed up for Keven and me that day. It mattered more than they could ever know.

When the service was over, I spent 10 more minutes alone with my beautiful boy. He was my reason for living—my love. I kissed his lips again; this time, my chest tightened, my throat burned. I swallowed the sobs that were begging to be released.

"Oh Keven, Keven, please give me signs that you're still with me." I had been begging him in my head for the last six days to communicate with me somehow. I knew this was my last moment with him physically; later today, my baby's body would be reduced to ashes. I didn't want to leave him! It was real—my son was gone.

My Beautiful Boy

CHAPTER 24
EARLY GRIEF

> *There is no "right" "way to grieve. Anything that somebody feels inside their own grief is correct.*
> ~Megan Devine

I was warned by other moms with shared experience that, after the memorial service, it would get quiet. Fewer people would check up on me, and eventually, most of the messages of support would end. They were right. I realized the reason for this had nothing to do with how people felt about me or my loss—they cared deeply. But they were uncomfortable around my grief.

This is not uncommon; in fact, in our culture, it seems like the norm. Friends and family want to see me move beyond Keven's death and for me to be happy again. It's painful for them to know that I'm suffering, and they want to help me get to the other side of grief and move on with life. Someone actually told me to "snap out of it" after three months! I didn't hold it against him; it was obvious that he sincerely thought he was helping me.

Having lost both parents, close family members, several close friends and Anthony, grief wasn't new to me. But all of those losses combined didn't come close to what losing Keven felt like. Therese and I cried on and off all day in the beginning, sometimes hysterically. My chest ached, my stomach hurt and my heart felt like broken shards of glass. Even if I managed to put the pieces back together, the centerpiece would always be missing. There would always be hollow space in my heart and life that only Keven could fill. The emptiness he left behind was enormous.

In those first days, it felt like part of Keven was still lingering around, especially in his room. The moment my hand turned the doorknob, my senses went into overdrive. Stepping in, I felt surrounded by his scent, like a warm embrace—I never wanted it to go away. Keven's bed was gone because it had been covered with his blood. His dirty clothes sat in one laundry basket and clean clothes in another. I buried my face in his T-shirts, crying, knowing that the scent would eventually fade.

Keven's beloved knife collection had shrunk because I'd let his closest friends take what was meaningful to them, and they all chose one of his knives. I had no intention of changing his room any time soon. Even now, over a year later, I still can't bring myself to clean it out.

Without Keven in the house, it was quiet, which was a constant reminder that he was gone. Every room held memories of something Keven had done or said over the last 29 years. The fridge was full of his favorite foods; a pack of his cigarettes was outside by the ashtray; TV shows he'd recorded were on the DVR; his favorite chair still smelled like him, and of course, his entire bedroom was now a shrine.

From the outside, I hadn't changed, but my inner self was being tossed by waves of grief. It was hard to breathe. There was a heaviness to my movements; everything around me was out of focus. I felt like I was suffocating. It started to feel as though the people in my life had forgotten about Keven and were unaware that my life as I knew it was over. Those first months felt like I was living in a different dimension of reality.

Peter left after 10 days. He took care of us and all the little details we couldn't see. We eventually broke up a few months later but are still friends. Once Peter was gone, it was back to doing everything for myself: housework, cooking, shopping—the mundane, daily life things that you do without really thinking. I felt nervous getting behind the wheel of my car. Being preoccupied with Keven's death meant I was distracted and unfocused.

As I walked into the grocery store the first time, I took my usual left turn down aisle four and stopped in front of the Rockstar energy drinks. I reached for one of the yellow cans, and the wind was knocked out of me. I would never need to buy these again. Keven was gone. Keven was not coming back. I began crying right there. Every aisle had something I would never buy again: blueberry Pop-Tarts, green apples, lemonade, ketchup. I was at another funeral.

In line, I recognized the checker. I had been going to this store for over 30 years and knew most of the employees—today, it was a sweet young lady named Lihn. Should I tell her? What if I cry? When she asked, "Hey, how are you doing today?" I told her between sobs about Keven. Lihn got tears in her eyes and said, "I want to hug you!" and because of COVID-19, she instead hugged herself. I gratefully accepted the sentiment. While it has become easier over time to shop in that store, it's still one of my least favorite places to go.

I'd also been going to the same small, family-owned pharmacy for over 30 years, and the main pharmacist, Ken, had been there for me through every new medication Keven took his entire life. They all knew Kev and were very fond of him. I received a sweet card from them on my doorstep when they heard the news. The first time I walked in after losing Kev, COVID or not, Ken came out from behind the counter and held me as I cried. He knew Keven was the center of my world. My favorite pharmacy tech was working that day, and he added, "I'll miss Keven, too. He was always so friendly and made me laugh." These are the things grieving parents live to hear.

Going out to run my normal errands became a dreaded task

because every clerk and cashier would ask the same innocent question: "How are you today?" I wished this nicety would just go away. Do I tell the truth or lie? The few times I answered honestly, it created an awkward moment for everyone within earshot. Nothing was the same, not even the simplest social exchanges. It was obvious how ill-prepared our culture is for dealing with grief.

Some people who haven't experienced child loss look at me differently. I imagine a parent that's lost a child to an illness or accident gets an immediate response of sympathy and compassion. Not always so when you say you've lost a son or daughter to overdose or suicide. I think most people feel sorry for me, but there are also those who judge both Keven and me; they are uncomfortable around me—even on social media. They don't know what to say, so they say nothing, which hurts even more than if they had said the wrong thing—or they say things to try to cheer me up. They offer advice without asking if I want it. They talk about the future too soon. They compare their grief experiences, even though they have not lost a child.

In my favorite book on grief, *It's OK That You're Not OK: Meeting Grief and Loss in a Culture That Doesn't Understand*, Megan Devine says, "The reality of grief is far different from what others see from the outside. There is pain in this world that you can't be cheered out of. You don't need solutions. You don't need to move on from your grief. You need someone to see your grief, to acknowledge it. You need someone to hold your hands while you stand there in blinking horror, staring at the hole that was your life. Some things cannot be fixed. They can only be carried."

I know that people are well-meaning and want to say the right thing when someone is grieving, so here is a shortlist of phrases to avoid:

I know how you feel. (No one knows exactly how someone feels.)

He's in heaven now. (This isn't comforting. I want him here with me.)

It was his/her time. (No, it wasn't! I'm supposed to die first—he was only 29!)

It was God's will/plan or *He was such a good person, God wanted him in heaven.* (Then I'm very angry with God for taking my only child.)

You'll be a much stronger, more compassionate person because of your loss. (I'm already very strong and compassionate.)

There's a reason for everything. (This makes me feel worse, not better.)

What can I do for you? (I appreciate the question, but I'm in a state of sorrow and can barely think straight.)

At least you have other children or can have more children. (This didn't apply to me, but I know a beautiful family with six children, and this was said to them often! As if their son didn't matter because they had other children!)

Some of these responses may seem harmless, and I'm guilty of using some myself. But when you think about it, you can see why these statements minimize the loss, bring the attention away from the deceased, try to justify the loss or assume you're going to get over the death.

Alternatively, here are some helpful, comforting things you can say or do:

You can grieve as long and hard as you need to, and I will be here for you. (Knowing someone understands is a huge comfort.)

I know how much you love (name). This must be so hard. (Please don't say "loved." Love doesn't end when the person dies.)

You're safe sharing anything with me. Do you want to talk about it? (Yes! I need to talk about it, and most people think talking about it hurts me. It hurts me to stay silent and pretend I'm fine.)

It's okay if you don't want to talk about it right now. I'm here to listen whenever. (This gives me permission to talk about it in the future.)

Can I make dinner/do laundry/run an errand for you/walk your dog? (Most people experiencing grief will not ask for help. Asking them what they need can feel overwhelming. Offer something specific because it's easier to accept.)

Give a food delivery gift card. (With apps like DoorDash, the grieving person can choose not only what they feel like eating but when. Appetites come and go in the beginning.)

Give a hug instead of speaking. (When one of my close friends lost her son five months before I lost Keven, we shared no words, just a long hug; words weren't needed.)

Offer to just sit with them with no pressure to have a conversation. (Sometimes, just having another person around helps.)

Ask *How are you feeling?* versus *Are you okay?* (I will never be "okay" again. I will find my new normal. Sometimes, even being asked how I'm feeling is too much.)

Send a card, gift, flowers or a plant. (I personally prefer a card. Flowers and plants require attention and care, and I can barely care for myself at this time.)

I was thinking of a memory of (name). Would you like to hear it? (Of course! I live for this now! Hearing good memories makes my day.)

Your son/daughter will be missed. (This touches my heart deeply.)

I'm sure you miss him/her so much. (Yes, I do, and this statement is a validation that you care.)

Find photos or videos you have of their lost loved one and give/send to them as soon as possible. Prepare a memorial video. There will never be a new photo or video, so receiving them from friends is priceless! (The photos and portraits I received of Keven from his friends are treasured gifts. It's like seeing him again.)

You've suffered the greatest type of loss there is. (Acknowledging the depth of the loss is validating and comforting. It's not like losing a parent or a spouse. As painful as those losses are, the pain of child loss goes deeper and never completely heals.)

I think about you and your son/daughter often. (It hurts to feel like everyone has forgotten your pain and your child. No matter how much time has passed, you're still grieving, and these words make a difference.)

Being a compassionate listener is just as important as figuring out exactly what to say. Try to listen with no judgment or suggestions. I've noticed it makes some people uncomfortable when I bring up Keven. I find myself not wanting to upset other people by talking about him, so if you are willing to listen, it's an appreciated gift! My friend, Virginia, did that for me recently, and afterward, I felt lighter for days. Her empathy soothed some of the pain. It was freeing to say what I was feeling and to feel heard. She never once tried to talk me out of my grief, and she gave me her full attention.

At gatherings or on holidays (especially their birthday and memorial date), acknowledge that the person is no longer here and is missed. If you avoid speaking about them, it feels like no one cares that he or she is gone or like they were never here. Saying something like, "If Keven were here, he'd be eating all the dinner rolls," can bring a smile.

When suicide is the cause of death, there are a few additional insensitive comments. I am offended when someone blames Keven for causing my grief. Yes, his death by suicide may appear selfish on the outside, but I never see it that way. I understand that more than anything, he needed to find peace after years of fighting his demons. He lived a tortured life for many years; watching his suffering was brutal. I can't imagine living the way Keven did.

Another common assumption is that the person who dies by suicide is weak, a coward or taking the easy way out. But that wasn't Keven. He was exhausted from fighting the war inside of himself, and he saw no hope in the future. I believe it took courage for him to pull that trigger and to make that final decision that it was his time to leave this world.

Receiving a text, especially from one of Keven's friends, is always a little thrill for me—even if it's just the three words, "I miss Keven." Ross, Andrew, Matt C. and Matt M. have done a good job staying in touch with me and sharing memories. One time when Ross was listening to one of Keven's favorite bands on the turntable Keven had given him, he snapped a photo and sent it to me. There was a Smashing Pumpkins album spinning and, right next to it, the little bottle of ashes I'd given Ross. It had me smiling for hours.

My friend Clyde makes a conscious effort to call me about once a month. He really wants to know how I'm holding up. It means so much to me. I always tell him the truth and typically laugh and cry during those conversations. My best friend, Kathy, and friends on Facebook have been a strong support system for me as well.

The biggest comfort for me is my Solace for Hope support group. Finding a group of people who share your experience is imperative for survival. The men and women in this group understand how I feel. We have a saying, "Say their name." Keven's name is music to my ears. I love hearing it. Most parents want their child mentioned and their name said aloud (or said in a message). Talking about him doesn't remind me of my loss—the loss is ingrained into my being. Talking about Keven is like saying, "I am aware that you've suffered the most traumatic loss imaginable. Your son mattered. He was special. I care about you."

I do my best to continue reaching out to the other grieving parents in Solace for Hope and other groups I've joined (specifically for suicide loss). I haven't stopped just because I'm hurting, too; it's more important to me now than ever to spread some love. Also, it's a reminder that the real me is still here, the compassionate part of me that cares about others.

We all deal with grief differently. Some people may think it's odd that I have Keven's ashes on the kitchen table where he would normally sit. To me, it's the center of the house, and he will always be the center of my life. I have mini memorials set up, too—one is next to the urn. It's a square, glass vase that holds Keven's glasses, watch, rings, wallet, keys and a few bracelets he wore all the time. In my bedroom, on a shelf, is the last Mother's Day gift and card he made me in 2020. Next to that is a glass jar filled with trinkets that remind me of him—his AA chips, a Cadillac emblem, a few more bracelets, a small ceramic heart he made for me and a little jar of Anthony's ashes. I have some of both their ashes sitting in the arms of a large ceramic angel on my dresser. I had a stuffed dog made from one of his shirts. I also carry some of his ashes in my purse in case I'm somewhere that he loved and have an opportunity to sprinkle some around. I got a tattoo on my right wrist that says, "Rest in Peace, Keven 1990–2020," with an infinity symbol and heart underneath. Every day I wear a necklace with his and Anthony's ashes, his fingerprint heart pendant and a charm with both of their birthstones.

Peter's daughter sent me a beautiful photo blanket with pictures of Kev when he was a kid. Another friend sent a windchime with his name engraved. My sweet friend Claudia gave me a leatherbound journal like the one she uses to write notes to Randy, the son she lost. All of these things are external ways of having Keven with me. Internally he's with me every second of every day.

The well-known psychiatrist, Elizabeth Kübler-Ross, named the five stages of grief: denial, anger, bargaining, depression and acceptance. These stages can happen in any order, at any time and may or may not happen for everyone experiencing grief. There is no one way, no right way and no wrong way to grieve. Kübler-Ross later noted that "the stages are not a linear and predictable progression" and that she regretted writing them in a way that was misunderstood.

There is another stage of grief that can happen in any loss but especially with overdose or suicide: guilt. Wondering what I could have done differently to save Keven haunts me. But it's not my fault. It's no one's fault in most cases. Most of us did everything in our power to save them, using only the tools at our disposal.

When guilt came up for me after Keven died, I had a long list of reasons for beating myself up. Maybe he wouldn't have died if I hadn't "helped" him so much. I was to blame that he didn't have a father. I was to blame for his access to a firearm. I was to blame for not figuring out a new way to help him. Letting go of the guilt is a process that I have to force myself to work through. I journal about it, share at meetings, and ultimately, I think I have finally forgiven myself and accepted that Keven's death was not my fault.

I know that I provided Keven with every type of help available and that I loved him unconditionally. I provided him a place to live where he was safe and taken care of. I tried everything, including tough love, and kicked him out for a time. So I believe that it's true that I did everything I could for him. Keven was determined to end his life. He would have done it sooner without my intervention. When he was ready, he found a way to leave, making sure he would not survive. My love could not save my son.

During the first few years of Keven's drug use, my life was out of control. Every waking moment, I had him in the back of my mind. Where was he? What was he doing? Did he steal anything from us today? Is he safe? Is he alive? Is he dead? I still have Keven in the back of my mind every moment, but there is a lot less stress. Yet I would go back to the stress and worry in a heartbeat if it would bring him back.

CHAPTER 25
LIFE AFTER KEVEN (16 MONTHS LATER)

> *Grieving the loss of a child begins on the day of your loss and ends on the day you are reunited.*
> ~Barbara Legere

They say time heals all wounds. I can tell you right now, that's not true. Time doesn't heal; it puts more distance between the pain and the present. For me, the intense pain I felt in the beginning is no longer my "normal," but there are days when it comes back like a sudden and unpredicted storm, knocking me back down and leaving me no choice but to lie on my bed curled up in a ball with my two dogs. I lost Sugar five months to the day of losing Keven, and it took two more to replace her. To honor Keven, I named one of them Chester B. (after Chester Bennington of Linkin Park, who also chose to end his life) and the other Evo (after Kev's first and favorite car, a Mitsubishi Lancer Evolution).

Living with a hole in your heart is not easy, but it's possible. You and I—we go on. Some days we want to die to escape the agony of the loss. Sometimes the pain is so unbearable we think we're going to die. Some days we feel pretty good. No matter what, we get up every morning and do it again. We get better at it as time goes on. We can socialize again, dance again, fall in love, give of ourselves, laugh and enjoy life. Losing a child is unlike any other loss because our children come from us—they are part of us. We mothers and fathers brought them into the world, and they were supposed to be here when we left, not the other way around.

Even though Keven's absence is a hole that will never heal, his memory is a blessing that fills me with warmth.

For me, the days are much easier than the nights. I can go through a day smiling and laughing and accomplishing my daily tasks. Now I can go to the store and not feel bothered by "have a nice day." By all appearances, I look like I'm doing fine. But as the sun descends on the horizon, I feel the light and the warmth leaving my heart. My memories aren't always of the good times. When I think of Keven suffering, I do my best to block it out, but if I see that suffering in my mind, even for one second, I can't bear it. The agonizing pain crushes my heart.

When my head hits the pillow each night, it's my time to "talk to Keven" before I fall asleep. I often cry in bed, which makes my dogs snuggle closer to me. I remember all the nights Kev came into my room to talk, to cry, to tell me about the voices in his head and his fear of being alone in his own room. Night-time is dark in more ways than one.

In the words of author Mitch Albom, "Death ends a life, not a relationship." Keven's gone from my physical world, but he's still very much part of my life. I can hear his voice sometimes, floating through time and space, saying, "I love you, Mom." Often when I'm doing something Keven and I did together (like watching certain TV shows), I have memories of exactly what he said or how his laugh sounded. He's alive in my thoughts and in my sister's, as well. We often joke about what Kev would say if he was still here because we know him so well. He's still my baby, my boy, my son. He will always be at the center of my life.

Writing this book has been therapeutic for me. My purpose was to share Keven's story in a way that would shed light on the stigma surrounding suicide and substance use, the challenges of getting treatment and to give a look into what it's like to be addicted to heroin and opiates. Mostly I wrote it to bring some comfort to those who are going through a similar loss. You are not alone. Contact a support group or email me directly and share your story (barbaralegere@gmail.com). If Keven's story helps one person, I will feel that I've accomplished my goal.

Though my journey through grief will never end, and the pain will never lessen, I will learn new ways to cope with my loss. There's a feeling of peace intertwined with the sadness because Keven's suffering is over. The new me—the person I became the moment I heard the gunshot—is growing and learning, and she's going to be okay.

I fought hard for Keven's sobriety—much harder than he did. He didn't want me to save him; he wanted me to love him where he was, and I did. While I had always loved him unconditionally, he couldn't feel love for himself. He felt shame and guilt and loathing. I made the decision to accept him and his choices (even though I didn't like them or agree with them). I gave him the respect that he didn't feel he deserved. I helped when he asked and kept my mouth shut when he didn't. It didn't change the outcome.

Although I made many mistakes along the way, I am at peace knowing that by following my instincts and loving Keven through it all, he knew how much I believed in him. He trusted and loved me until the very end. And by giving my son permission to die, I gave him the freedom he needed—freedom from his pain—something I could not give him in life. Keven had to die to be free.

Me and Keven, Christmas 2010

IN MEMORIAM

Over the course of Keven's struggles with substance use, our lives were touched by countless others who faced the same demons. Too many of them were taken too soon by drugs. They were brave even though they were in pain and causing pain. They were and are loved. Just like Keven, they mattered.

Here is an incomplete list of many of the people we knew or knew of. Most of these loved ones are from the Solace for Hope family. Below is a link to Solace for Hope's memorial video tribute, to see some of the beautiful faces of those listed below:

https://youtu.be/n2wFKD0Vz48

Nolan James Smith - Forever 15
Christopher Michael Ritchie - Forever 16
Mark Melkonian - Forever 17
Connor Jack Roberts - Forever 18
Alexander Joseph Marks - Forever 19
Christopher Joseph Straughn - Forever 19
Harley Swank - Forever 19
Benjamin Dunkle - Forever 20
Christopher A. Love - Forever 20
Malik Isaiah Dufor - Forever 20
Charles Nicholas Vanoff - Forever 20

Casey Thompson - Forever 21

Christian Jack Taylor - Forever 21

Aaron Sylla - Forever 22

Heather Marie Trott - Forever 22

Kaelyn Tomsen - Forever 22

Mitchell Craig Fleitman - Forever 22

Eric Christopher Pierson - Forever 23

Samuel Pantaleon - Forever 23

Torin Wood - Forever 23

Brandon Tyler Tucker - Forever 24

Danny Contreras - Forever 24

Daniel Donovan Lewis - Forever 25

Jayson Garland-Mocnik - Forever 25

Justin R. Guittar - Forever 25

Lauren Montgomery - Forever 25

Ryan David Rapp - Forever 25

Tyler Scott Eigelbach - Forever 25

Ethan Jerome Berkowitz - Forever 26

Henry Isaac Brown - Forever 26

Ian Christopher Jones - Forever 26

Ryan Michael Mramer - Forever 26

Andrew Alexander D'Paraschi Togo - Forever 27

Anthony Edward Pugh - Forever 27

Donnie Lace III - Forever 27

Jay Phillip Flamm - Forever 27

Justin Michael Logan - Forever 27

Nicholas Michael Nama - Forever 27

Todd Anthony Campbell - Forever 27

William (Willie) Aaron-Anthony Ayala - Forever 27

Riley Alan Ward - Forever 28

Ryan Keith Hill - Forever 28

Sky Ambruster - Forever 28

Tyler Jeremy Terry - Forever 28

Alexander Jack Arens - Forever 29

Keven David Legere - Forever 29

Scott Austin Cortes - Forever 29

Trevor James Manning - Forever 29

Darren "Cliff" Piccirillo - Forever 30

Joel "Joey" Abraham Cymerint - Forever 30

Kevin Michael Fortin - Forever 30

Noah Naderzad - Forever 30

Toby Markes - Forever 30

Brian Richard Schickling - Forever 31

Christopher Paul Don - Forever 31

Shane Eric Hoke - Forever 31

Brandon Luke Smith - Forever 32

Julia Ann May - Forever 32

Jessica Anne May - Forever 33

Randy Jones - Forever 34

Sadie Jones - Forever 34

Adam Levi Throp - Forever 35

Aaron James Lanari (AJ) - Forever 35

Bryan Berry - Forever 36

Nathaniel Craig Hill - Forever 36

Adrian Gayle Beaney - Forever 37

Damien Robert Repasi - Forever 41

Alisa Marie Hicks - Forever 44

Brent Keith Burrows - Forever 62

KEVEN'S POETRY

While Keven was struggling with substance use, he turned to creative outlets like poetry. Though the poems he wrote are dark, I'm including some of them here for additional insight into the pain and difficulty of what he was experiencing.

HOW FAR CAN YOU GET

They say suicide is for cowards
But let's see how far you get
Holding your head to a railroad track trying to forget
Or the barrel in your mouth finger itching on the trigger
Let's see how many pills you take before you can't remember
Let's see how long it takes you to jump with a noose around
your neck
But seriously, let's see how far you get

BROKEN

Each time my heart breaks
It becomes harder to heal
And hope fades
Into desolation
Loneliness and despair
Which turns to self hatred and self loathing
But soon It will be over
But soon it will end
Because I found you my only friend
Bang, bang now I'm dead

AN ODE TO HEROIN

You are the one for me
You are my one and only
You are my one and only
But you don't love me
You really despise me
From innocent eyes
You give me false intention
From which my hatred rises
I need you now more than ever
But you mock me through your black veil
You are by my side
Again the cold leaves
Now you are gone
You left me so quickly
The sickness returns without you
You are the only one for me
You are my one and only
You are all I need

LIFE

Let's see how many attempts there are
Before we see success
Remember it only takes once
For the rope to snap your neck
Does money make you happy?
Actually I wouldn't know
Cause if I ever had any
I'd spend it all on dope
Can't find what you're looking for
I can surely understand
Cause I can't seem to find
This vein in my hand

SHORT AND SWEET

Around me the world turns
As I slowly burn
The pain does not subside
I should give up and die

COME ON DOWN

Come one come all
Come on down
It's not something I want at all
For I know what is there and I am scared
For the pain filled with cold chills
Come down from there you are too high
But the fall is far too great
And surely from this I will break
The sleepless nights the endless aches
I know I cannot take
So I will stay high up here
In these black liquid clouds
From here I watch this bloody mushroom cloud erupt

BROKEN AND FRAYED

I won't tell a soul
That I'm mad as hell
Torn broken and frayed
I am torn broken and frayed
No I'm cold worn out and shamed

LEAVE

You need to leave
You need to go
With you here
Great horror unfolds
When you're gone it gets much worse
For surely soon I'll be in a Hearse
But only if you don't leave
Although the pain will
Stop for the day
I still pray you go away

BLANK PAGE

Blank page is all the rage
Got in my car and killed myself today
185 on the freeway
Blank page is all the rage
Let's shoot up and kill ourselves today
Too much H in my veins
Blank page is all the rage
Stuck in jail too many days
Can't stand my cellmates
Why can't you see my rage?
Can't you see it on my face?
Can't you tell I'm not okay?
I wrote it all on this blank page
Blank page is all the rage
I felt myself slip away
Why don't I feel the same?
I know I am not okay
I feel too much pain
From all this blank rage

END OF GOODBYE

I say goodbye to the stars, the clouds, the suns
And the moons
I wish many
Good things to you
For I will not see any of you again my friends
But you say I can see you anywhere anytime
But I say this I cannot see any of you
Beneath the earth where I'll be for eternity
For I decided this, that by choice I will end my life

ZERO

I am nothing to this world
Just an empty hole immersed
The books I read
The shows I watched
To my soul they cannot touch
The windows are glazed
From where I stand
To everyone I cry in despair
I am nothing
I am zero

ACKNOWLEDGMENTS

Therese, you held our bundle of joy before I did. You were by my side from the moment Keven entered this world up to the moment he left it. A bond formed between you and "the boy" that was both precious and fun. You weren't just an aunt to him; you were the good cop to my bad, the sibling he always longed for, his cohort and the only other person he trusted completely. From dinosaurs to driving to drugs, your love for him never skipped a beat. You listened, laughed and cried. He was proud to introduce you to his friends as his "cool aunt." T, Keven loved you with his entire heart and felt your love for him. "Thank you for being there" doesn't cover how much your presence in his life means to me. I know you wouldn't have wanted it any other way.

Sister Margaret, your special bond with Keven was beautiful and touching. Knowing how much he was loved and prayed for by his great-aunt meant so much to both of us. You loved him unconditionally, and he knew it.

To my brother, David, and his family: Dave, Cindy, Liara, Landon, Danielle, Joel, Wyatt, Alexa, Ryan and Mireya. Thank you for your love and support. Keven loved each of you even though he couldn't always express it.

Kathy Scruton, if it weren't for you, I never would have met "Jim," and Keven never would have been born! Thank you for that and for being my BFF since way back in high school. Not everyone is lucky enough to have such a great friend and confidante. Even from afar, you are with me every day, and your encouragement has kept me going on some of my darkest days. Love you!

Peter Heymans, you knew Keven better than any of my other friends. Thank you for knowing exactly how to engage him in a conversation that would light up his smile (and get him talking nonstop for an hour!). Thank you for dropping everything and driving the seven hours down here to be with me when I called and let you know he was gone. Your love and support have been invaluable.

Thank you, Glen Woolsey, for our over 20-year friendship. You've been there for a lot of what I went through with Keven and gave me comfort and encouragement. Distance is irrelevant for us. I love you.

Sherry Calvert, you are and always will be one of my closest friends. Who would have thought two women who lived on opposite coasts and were seemingly so different from each other would become so close? You've always been here for me, and I cherish you and our special bond. (Chester B and Evo say "Hi" to Wren.)

To Heidi Le—thank you for simply being *you*. You're a beautiful, purple shining star who makes my life brighter. You're an exceptional human being, and I'm blessed to have you in my life.

William Gonzalez—you were a good friend to Keven and still are to me. Even while inside prison walls, you've managed to have my back. We've been there for each other for years as we've endured the ups and downs of life. Thank you for your loving presence. (Next book will be about you!)

My "To Be Determined with Serenity" girls: Annette Taber-Marshall, Tori Lee, Joy Bury, Denise James and Dawn McCoy (RIP), you heard it all and then some. You walked in my shoes alongside me when Keven was here. I hope and pray you never walk in my current shoes. I love you and your children and am forever grateful for your friendship.

Maggie Fleitman and every person involved with Solace for Hope: thank you. Whether our loved one is still here or has passed on, we walk in shoes that no one wants to wear. By sharing our words, time and compassion, we have a safe and loving place. Thank you, Maggie, for giving so much of your time and your heart to create this community.

Clyde Taber, thanks for making a point of checking in on me and always faithfully reading my blog! You've listened to me laugh and cry and always with an open and loving heart. You and your family will always be in my heart.

Monica Rulon, Lori Cote and Matt Cardinale—thank you for providing me with excellent input whenever I got stuck! The book is better because of your insights. I felt safe sharing with you, and your brilliance helps my book shine.

Blog friends! I remember way back when blogging was new, and people thought I was crazy for calling you my "friends" since we'd never met in person. Some of you are better friends to me than my "face-to-face" friends. I could not have survived the first few years of Keven's substance use without your compassion, concern, information and honesty. Thank you to Adrienne Blinn, Aphra Rogers, Bob & Ann Edwards, Donna Van Horn, Fay Akers, Helga Culbert, Jeff Jacobson, Jessica Obenschain, Jim & Michelle Romano, Karen Davidenko, Kathy Kostelnick, Lacey Suarez, Lori Cote, Linda Lou, Lisa Carp, Lora Erickson, Monica Rulon, Mike & Robyn Welsh, Peggy Ludwig, Renee Vezeau-Kennedy, Ron Grover, Shawna Pierson and Sherri Smith.

Keven's friends: Ross Salzberg, Andrew Scott, Matt Cardinale, Matt Mattice and Jesse Young. You guys helped me so much during the first few months of grief. You carry memories and stories of Keven that no one else knows. Each time you give me a nugget from the past, it feels like a warm hug from Kev himself. While he was here, he was your friend, your brother. He wasn't always easy to be around, but he knew who his real friends were, and so do I. John Horn, you were one of his true friends. Thank you so much for attending his memorial service; it touched my heart.

To Keven's SUD specialist physician, Dr. Bruce Seligsohn—

Keven told me you were the one man he could be himself with. He listened to you and felt validated by you—something he got very little of. He respected you deeply. I'm grateful not just for the medical help but for your generosity and kindness toward my boy. I will never forget how your presence in his life helped him to keep trying.

To Anthony's friends who have kept his memory alive and have become women I admire and love, Presley & Gabrielle Graham, Cheryl Fultz, Kelli Hillman and Cheyanne Engle Smith. Your friendship is a gift.

Thank you, Anna David, Founder of Legacy Launch Pad Publishing, for saying to me "you have a book!" and giving me the courage to move forward. I continue to learn from your ever-flowing fountain of knowledge. And a huge thank you for introducing me to the Inner Circle writing group!

To Halina, Kaitlin and Ryan—my Legacy Launch Pad team—your edits, insights and creativity helped this book be the best that it could be. It was such a joy working with you and benefitting from your expertise. You took so much stress out of this process! Halina—your insight and professional takes on each chapter were invaluable. I'm so grateful you were my editor!

To the Inner Circle writing group (past and present), I did it! Without you guys and gals, I might still be fumbling around trying to get the first chapter out. You are my peeps, my Brady Bunch square family! Each of you is an amazing person I am privileged to know. You've encouraged me and taught me along the way. I love every one of you. I wish I could name you all, but you know who you are—especially the core group of us that keeps showing up day after day! *You rock my world!* Thank you sincerely for your presence in my life.

Last but never least, to Chester B and Evo. Your constant companionship, affection and loyal love get me through each day. You're Mommy's good boys and I love you so much!

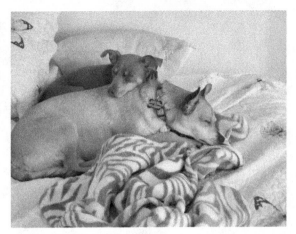

Chester B and Evo

RESOURCES

RESOURCES

Solace for Hope Foundation:
https://solaceforhope.org/

Al-Anon:
https://al-anon.org/

Alcoholics Anonymous:
https://www.aa.org/

FACEBOOK GROUPS:

Solace for Hope Compassion Group:
https://www.facebook.com/groups/solaceorangecounty

Moms for All Paths to Recovery from Addiction @ Heart of a Warrior Woman:
https://www.facebook.com/groups/822048691486320

Challenges, Inc. Harm Reduction Group:
https://www.facebook.com/groups/challengesinc

Faces of Opioids—Stories of Using, Death and Recovery:
https://www.facebook.com/groups/facesofopioids

The Fentanyl Awareness Coalition:
https://www.facebook.com/groups/195408679079701

Meth Addiction Recovery and Family Support:
https://www.facebook.com/groups/514389019735187

Helping Parents Heal—Moving Forward After Suicide:
https://www.facebook.com/groups/HPHmovingfor-
wardaftersuicide

BOOKS

The Problem of Pain by C.S. Lewis (1940, Harper One)

The Effects of Childhood Trauma on Adult Perception and Worldview by Asa Don Brown (January 2011, Proquest, Umi Dissertation Publishing)

The Single-Parent Family: Living Happily in a Changing World by Marge Kennedy and Janet Spencer King (1994, Three Rivers Press)

Grace (Eventually): Thoughts on Faith by Anne Lamott (February 2008, Riverhead Books)

Traffick by Ellen Hopkins (November 2015, Margaret K. McElderry Books)

In the Realm of Hungry Ghosts by MD Gabor Maté (January 2010, North Atlantic Books)

A Common Struggle: A Personal Journey Through the Past and Future of Mental Illness and Addiction by Patrick J. Kennedy, Stephen Fried (Blue Rider Press)

Smile Anyway: Quotes, Verse, and Grumblings for Every Day of the Year by Richelle E. Goodrich (June 2015, CreateSpace Independent Publishing Platform)

I Am a Heroin Addict by Ritchie Farrell (May 2017, Create-Space Independent Publishing Platform. Previously published as *What's Left of Us* May 2017)

In Her Words: On Women, Politics, Leadership and Lessons from Life by Eleanore Roosevelt (September 2017, Black Dog & Leventhal)

This Is Gonna Hurt: Music, Photography, and Life Through the Distorted Lens of Nikki Sixx by Nikki Sixx (April 2011, Harper Collins)

Wake Up and Smell the Coffee!: Advice, Wisdom, and Uncommon Good Sense by Ann Landers (May 1998, Villard)

Chicken Soup for the Teenage Soul by Jack Canfield, Mark Victor Hansen, Kimberly Kirberger (August 2012, Back-list, LLC)

American Fix: Inside the Opioid Addiction Crisis—and How to End It by Ryan Hampton (August 2018, All Points Books)

The Giving Tree by Shel Silverstein (October 1964, Harper and Row)

It's OK That You're Not OK: Meeting Grief and Loss in a Culture That Doesn't Understand by Megan Devine (October 2007, Sounds True, Inc.)

ABOUT THE AUTHOR

 Barbara Legere is a writer and contributor to the bestselling book *The Epiphanies Project*. As an advocate for those suffering from substance use disorders, mental health issues and grief, she has been featured in *Salon* and *The Huffington Post*. Legere lives in Southern California with her sister, Therese, as well as her two dogs, cat and tortoise. Her writing can be found on barbaralegere.com. *Keven's Choice* is her first book.